HIGH COOKERY

GILAD MEIRI

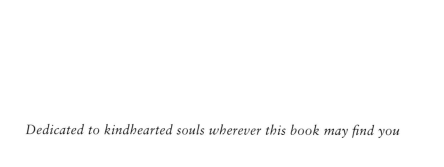

Dedicated to kindhearted souls wherever this book may find you

HIGH COOKERY

Your Guide for Cannabis Cooking
and the Munchies

GILAD MEIRI

PUBLISHED
IN
04/20

HIGH COOKERY

Your Ultimate Guide for the Munchies

Gilad Meiri

www.highcookery.com

Photography: Assaf Ronen

Visual Design & Website Design: Studio Tamar Bar Dayan, Nawal Arafat

Food Styling: Naama Ran

Fashion & Outdoor Styling: Sheera Hoekman

Editing: Perrin Davis

Proofreading: Katie Jones-Aiello

Models: Bia Gott, Jeremie Kleiner, Yael Meiri, Yoav Meiri, Nitzan Shitay,

Cole Duerr, Hila Richany, Maayan Korman, Matan Rabizadeh,

Yosi Mizrachi, Hadar Vaknin

Authored in California, Printed in Canada

First Printing, 2020

ISBN 978-1-7333662-0-5

www.highcookery.com

Thanks!

This book is the result of a wonderful journey of nearly two years. It started, like many great creations, with a cannabis-infused idea. My friend WhyTai and I planted the seed, and in the weeks that followed, it grew into a meaningful sapling.

Many people took part in making this book happen starting from brainstorming sessions; hours of cooking; several dozen fun meetups of tasting and testing with like-minded people; and production, photography, styling, editing, and design sessions. I could go on and on.

I'd like to give special thanks to my wife, Daphne, who suffers through all my crazy ideas. She above all knows what it's like when I have a project I'm passionate about—the endless work hours, the preoccupied weekends, the attention diverted from so many other commitments. Yet for some undecipherable reason, she puts up with it, and for that, among others, I'm eternally grateful.

Tzipi, Nitzan, Yael and Yoav, thank you so much for rolling up your sleeves and being there for all the cooking days and photoshoots. It would have taken me twice the time and generated only half the fun if you hadn't been there!

To Nava, my mother-in-law, who donated (not to mention sacrificed) her dwellings for this book's photoshoots and culinary experimentation – my eternal appreciation!

This book is the brainchild of Ytai/WhyTai Ben-Tsvi, and me. We were both there, sharing a joint, when the notion was conceived, and he remained at my side throughout the frustrations, debates, and tedious pixel work. Thank you!

To create this book, I was fortunate enough to assemble a team of the best of the best: Assaf Ronen, the best food photographer I've ever seen; Na'ama Ran, an amazing food stylist who shaped each dish to its fullest potential; Tamar Bar Dayan, a graphic designer to rule them all—I am still inspired by your ability to conceive such phenomenal works of art; and of course Perrin Davis and katie Jones-Aiello who successfully transformed my jibber-jabber into a coherent text.

Throughout the process, I've asked many good people to contribute their time, attention, critical thinking, and taste buds. I am so grateful to have been surrounded by and to have access to such beautiful beings. I'm truly humbled by their willingness to help: Gabriella Meiri; Zeevik Meiri; Tali (Boobooit) Brauman; Sagy (Booboo) Volkov; Ya'ara Ben-Tsvi; Asaf and Liad Sadowski; Ziv Sol; Avi Fashali; Manor Hemel; Carmit Jacobson; Jane Snyder, Edva and Amir Biner-Levy; Elena Molchanova; Nick Salloum; Pamela Desrochers; Carsten Bergmann; Lauren Peetz; Gianpaolo Lisi; and Efrat and Yaniv Katan.

Part I:

CANNA COOKING

Part II:

COOKING FOR THE MUNCHIES

THIS BOOK:
WHAT IT'S ALL ABOUT

Marijuana is rapidly becoming legitimate. What was once a half-hidden college experience is slowly transitioning into the mainstream. Legalization of marijuana is a hot topic, and many people are now giving it a try, after realizing that weed is neither a gateway drug nor is it harmful when consumed responsibly.

Food and cannabis are tightly connected, first and foremost because most of us consume food while under the influence, and second because food enhanced with marijuana (referred to as edibles) is among the best carriers of THC, the component responsible for the euphoric high.

However, for various reasons, consumption of cannabis has been stereotypically connected with junk food. Maybe it was because of the renegade nature of smoking, or maybe it was because smoking weed was associated with the so-called, "potheads" who had nonexistent culinary threshold. Whatever the reason, it's time we up the game.

Whether you're a foodie, a health-conscious person, or, like me, a person who sees cooking as a truly enjoyable and meditative practice, this book is for you. I don't accept the idea that one should have to lower the quality of the experience by eating junk food. It takes away from the adventure and will fill you with regret afterward.

Being high should be looked at as an opportunity. Food is not merely a means to satisfy the munchies. It can be an essential part of your adventure. When you're high, your senses work differently. You appreciate things more easily; you're more creative and imaginative. Don't limit yourself to processed, industrialized, packaged food. If something should be avoided, it's the unpronounceable ingredients in junk food. So light up a joint and your gas stove, and get cooking!

Enjoy, Gilad

MARIJUANA AND FOOD

THE CONNECTION, BOTH HISTORICAL AND TODAY

Today, the most common method of consuming cannabis is through various forms of smoking or vaping. But for most of recorded history, that was not the case. In ancient times, eating or drinking cannabis were the predominant means of consumption. Historians have found instances of cannabis- and hashish-based foods going back centuries in China, India, and the Middle East.

In the US, cannabis extracts dissolved in an alcohol solution were widely sold in pharmacies until the late 1960s to be used for the alleviation of pain, stomach disorders, and depression. In fact, pretty much the main thing that has changed regarding marijuana edibles is their legal status. The concept of smoking weed didn't become "fashionable" in the US until the early twentieth century.

While pot slowly inched its way into the mainstream mindset, food has evolved significantly in past decades. In the 1960s and 1970s, creativity in cooking had a massive boost, as spices, flavors, and cooking methods from various cultures were widely embraced. Alongside plain old bacon, eggs, and potatoes, we began to enjoy curries, chutneys, and soufflés.

The slow re-legalization of marijuana and its increased legitimacy among the public, along with decades of culinary creativity and experimentation, have revived the canna-cooking phenomenon; fortunately, now canna-cooking is enjoying a phenomenal boost in attention. This in turn has driven innovation and increased access to quality ingredients. In short, the future is bright, so feel free to jump on the wagon!

WEED AND FOOD: FACTS AND FICTION

Let's critically examine some of the myths surrounding cannabis and food.

MYTH #1:

Eating the flower will get you high. Reality: Wrong.

The only thing eating the raw flower will get you is an immediate need for mouthwash. Raw cannabis contains THCa, which has great anti-inflammatory and neuroprotective properties but doesn't intoxicate you like THC. To transform THCa to its euphoric counterpart, you'll need to infuse the cannabis into a carrier: mostly fat (butter or oil) or alcohol (tinctures). Doing so requires weed to undergo the essential stage of decarboxylation (see page 22).

MYTH #2:

The munchies are just in your head. Reality: Wrong.

Here's hoping that this little tidbit alleviates some of the guilt associated with the munchies: They're more than just a stereotype. Marijuana hijacks the part of the brain that controls hunger. The neurons that are responsible for shutting down eating promote hunger while you're high on weed.

MYTH #3:

It is possible to know the potency of an edible. Reality: Partially true.

Technology has allowed us to get a much better handle on the potency of edibles. However, finding out the true potency of an edible is a long and expensive process. The science is still in its infancy and differs depending on different preparation methods and types of food. Different brands offer different guesstimates, but trial and error are still your safest bet.

MYTH #4:

You can OD on edibles. Reality: Wrong.

Edibles can definitely deliver an unpleasant experience and can have a serious negative psychological effect. However, in terms of toxicity, it is virtually impossible for an adult to ingest a lethal dose. Just for the sake of comparison, a person who consumes 10 times the recommended serving of alcohol per body weight is in a lethal danger zone, while a person who consumes 10,000 times the amount of THC contained in an average joint will still be in good physical health (obviously, I wouldn't recommend going there, though).

Myth #5:

The munchies make you eat junk food. Reality: Partially true.

Kale salad or pizza and Oreos? When you're high and hit that munchies stage, your brain sounds the hunger alarm. Instinct and evolution push your seemingly starving body to seek out high-fat and high-calorie foods.

Myth #6:

No one can get addicted to weed. Reality: Wrong.

While marijuana is not nearly as addictive as cigarettes or alcohol, some people do develop a dependency. Studies have varied, but somewhere between 9 percent and 17 percent of users develop some level of dependency, which can impact motivation and ambition. The good news, however, is that getting clean and even returning to moderate and responsible habitual use is relatively easier than with cigarettes or alcohol.

Myth #7:

Consuming weed on an empty stomach increases your high. Reality: Wrong.

There is no evidence showing that smoking or eating weed on an empty stomach versus a full one will affect your high. That said, your body diverts a lot of energy to digestion, so once you start eating—especially if you're munching endlessly—you will get increasingly tired, which can definitely impact the quality of your high.

Infusions

Sweet High of Mine

Savory and Intoxicating

CANNA
COOKING

Edible marijuana is a great medium to help you experience a full-body euphoric sensation. Personally, I've enjoyed some of my most pleasant and insightful marijuana-induced adventures when experimenting with edibles. That said, if you're new to this mode of consumption, start slow, as it can get intense (read the intro to this chapter).

Using cannabis as an ingredient naturally takes food to a whole different level. The world of canna-cooking uses edibles either as a means of ingesting the substance or as an essential part of the flavor profile of a dish. Personally, I don't find that cannabis positively affects the taste of dishes, so I focus my culinary attention on disguising the taste as much as possible. Cooking with cannabis can be a lot of fun, and the taste and impact is definitely different than store-bought edibles. You are much more in charge of the taste, strain quality, and dosage.

Once you infuse an ingredient with cannabis, you can pretty much transform any recipe into a 'canna-recipe'. If your recipe doesn't have a fatty ingredient, like butter or oil, just sprinkle some drops of THC tincture over it, and you have yourself a "special" version.

EDIBLES VS. SMOKING

Compared to inhaling cannabis, edibles produce a different effect. Some would say that ingesting marijuana brings about a much stronger high, and some of them would be right. However, a more accurate description would be that the two effects are just different.

When weed is ingested, the cannabinoids are processed through the liver before they enter your brain. In the liver, the delta-9-THC is metabolized into 11-hydroxy-THC, which is a fancy way of saying that the liver transforms some of the drug's active ingredients. Cannabis that is absorbed through the lungs goes straight to the brain.

So despite the fact that ingested cannabis typically delivers a smaller dose of cannabinoids, the high may be much stronger. This newly transformed substance produces a more psychedelic experience. This translates differently in different people, but generally speaking, an edible high is described as a "body high," which means that users feel a much more intense and body-numbing experience. This is also why overdoing it with edibles may bring about a negative and somewhat hallucinogenic adventure.

Another main difference is timing. When smoking or vaping, you will feel an immediate effect that dissipates within two hours. Edibles, on the other hand, must go through the digestive system and typically take one to two hours (or in my case, three) to produce a high. However, an edible high will last significantly longer—sometimes up to ten hours. People who use marijuana for medicinal purposes often prefer oral ingestion because they don't have to consume as often.

Read This If You've Yet to Experiment with Edibles

As I mentioned above, ingesting cannabis has the potential to cause unpleasant experiences if done wrong. In fact, I know many people who have either explored their boundaries or went about eating weed wrong and experienced a bad result. To their credit, this mistake typically happens only once, as people tend to learn quickly.

The good news is that unlike with alcohol or some other drugs, there is no long-term potential harm in the vast majority of cases. It is virtually impossible for an adult to consume a lethal cannabis overdose.[1] However, if you do feel distressed after taking edibles, it is best to seek company and alert others to the fact you're not feeling safe. This will help you deal with potential panic and confusion.

If this is your first time, start slow. Eat just a bit (5mg to 10mg) and wait for at least two hours. Check your watch, and do not eat any more edibles before the full two-hour period has passed. The main reason why people consume too much is impatience. If you must have instant gratification, vape or smoke, but don't eat any more.

[1.] *In his book "Weed: The User's Guide," David Schmader calculated that a lethal overdose would require eating 1,500 pounds of cannabis in 15 minutes.*

STORING EDIBLES AROUND KIDS

Now that cannabis is gaining both social and legal legitimacy, kids are more frequently seeing marijuana in relaxed settings. Whether you decide to consume weed in the presence of children or to conceal it, you must take precautions when storing your stash around kids. While cannabis is not really toxic to adults, it does pose a real threat to kids. As the prevalence of its use increases, so are the reports of infants, toddlers, and kids ingesting joint buds or edibles. It is important to emphasize that this can be extremely harmful and potentially lethal. If you suspect that a child has ingested cannabis, you must seek medical care immediately.

The best strategy, obviously, is to act responsibly and be very careful about how you store, mark, and dispose of your cannabis. The industry is constantly introducing innovative storage solutions that prevent kids from accessing what's inside. If you are a habitual user, the best thing would be to find one of these solutions and use it religiously.

However, even if you're not going for a dedicated solution, make sure to clearly mark edibles and store them in the most difficult-to-access spot you can find. When you're finished eating or smoking, make sure you clean up any crumbs or buds and throw them in the trash.

COOKING WITH CANNABIS: BEYOND THE BROWNIE

I can't count the times people have asked me what edibles exist beyond the brownie. Which begs the question: How did the brownie get a stranglehold on its title as the ultimate edible? Intuitively, I guess, tradition plays a significant role; however, the practical reason is that chocolate very effectively disguises the flavor of marijuana.

The medical marijuana industry, seeing the commercial potential in introducing other flavors and forms, has jumped on the culinary bandwagon and has begun to introduce more varieties of edibles. Their efforts have contributed significantly to the "canna-chef" or "ganja gourmet" phenomenon.

Today, you can find all kinds of "happy" and intoxicating recipes, from desserts to salads to slow-cooked casseroles to cocktails. Some canna-chefs have diverted their efforts away from concealing the taste of cannabis and now embrace the flavor profile, thus introducing culinary styles that incorporate and even emphasize its bitter, herbal flavor.

That said, I still find that most people choose to eat their cannabis not as part of a gourmet experience but rather as an edible vehicle that'll help chase down a bitter pill. Therefore, even though it's not all about brownies, you will see in the recipes I present that sweet tastes are still the bread and "budder" of edible marijuana.

A Bit about CBD and THC

Both cannabidiol and tetrahydrocannabinol, conveniently abbreviated as CBD and THC, are compounds found in cannabis. Think of CBD as THC's nerdy friend. While THC is notorious for being the essential ingredient responsible for cannabis's exhilarating high, CBD offers many benefits, too—just without the buzzy sensation.

Chemically, the two compounds have an almost identical molecular structure with a slight variance in their arrangement of atoms. This variance causes different psychoactive impacts on the body. But make no mistake—both CBD and THC interact easily with the brain's cannabinoid receptors and have tremendous health benefits.

Users who prefer to enjoy the medicinal prowess of marijuana without the high often focus their attention on CBD-rich strains. CBD has shown to have a positive impact on various health issues, such as enhancement of energy levels; alleviation of pain; treatment of chronic illnesses; and reduction of anxiety, depression, and symptoms related to cancer.

Cooking with CBD is almost identical to cooking with THC. Both need a fat- or alcohol-based carrier used as a "regular" ingredient in the cooking process. If you wish your carrier to be CBD-predominant, you'll need to use a strain with high CBD content and low THC content; you can typically find such strains in any dispensary.

The only difference when cooking with CBD is the decarboxylation process. Decarbing CBD requires a higher temperature than THC due to the CBD compound's higher boiling point. Check out the decarboxylation tutorial on page 22.

INFUSING FOODS WITH CANNABIS: START HERE

DECARBOXYLATION

Whether you're in it just for the joy of exploring and cooking, or you're health conscious and don't care for heavy use of the processed ingredients that are present in most off-the-shelf edibles, you'll find cooking with cannabis fun and rewarding. Similar to cooking with wine, the quality of the ingredient does affect the end result. I'm not saying that you need to use the absolute best strains, but don't assume you can use low-quality leftovers and get the desired result.

The herb by itself is not ingestible. Do not try to chew the flower; it won't get you high, and you'll need a heavy dose of mouthwash afterward. In order for cannabis to have an intoxicating effect in edibles, it needs to be infused into a carrier, typically one that is alcohol or fat based. This is why most cannabis-boosted recipes use tinctures or various forms of butter or oil.

After you've picked up your strain and crushed it finely (a regular crusher is fine, but an electric spice grinder is better), the next step is decarboxylation. I'll give you a minute to make sure you've read that correctly...

For cannabis to have an intoxicating effect, two conditions must be met: the flower must be both dried and heated. Decarboxylation means exactly that. By heating the dried flower (or drying and heating it at the same time), you activate the THC and release its euphoric powers.

The trick to decarboxylating weed is to use the lowest heat possible that's still hot enough to be effective. High heat degrades the herb and takes away some of its effect. It's an easy and very essential process:

1| Preheat your oven to 230°F (for CBD decarbing, please see the following comment*). Make sure you're using the turbo (fan) setting, for the most even spread of the heat. If you know that your oven typically requires a higher heat setting than recommended in recipes, go as high as 240°F, but no hotter.

2| Line a baking sheet with parchment paper and spread the ground and dried flower evenly.

3| Bake for 50 minutes, stirring the plant material every 15 minutes or so. Remove from the oven and set aside, covered, until it cools completely.

4| That's it—you're ready to infuse!

*For CBD decarboxylation, make sure you use a CBD-predominant strain. Follow the same process, but preheat the oven to 245°F and bake for 70 minutes (it needs to be hotter because CBD compounds have a higher boiling point).

WHAT STRAINS SHOULD YOU USE?

Marijuana flowers come in numerous strains, but are generally divided into three groups:

SATIVA

Believed to provide a more uplifting, cerebral high that doesn't take away from the user's energy level, Sativa is a common choice for daytime smoking or smoking at social gatherings.

INDICA

Believed to deliver a more physically numbing high, Indica is often used at night for relaxation.

HYBRID

Containing some ratio of both Sativa and Indica, it may resemble one more than the other, depending on the characteristics it inherits from the parent strains.

I've used the word "believed" in the above descriptions, as there's no real data that suggests the above is true. Even though some say the experiences of using Sativa and Indica are vastly different, I personally never felt it. Remember that energy levels and context also play a major role in how your adventure will shape up.
If you have a favorite strain for vaping or smoking, I'd recommend using it in recipes as well. If you're making edibles to achieve a euphoric high, it's best to be safe and use strains with low levels of CBD, as some chefs claim THC and CBD seem to work against each other when cooking, though that's far from scientifically established.

DETERMINING THE POTENCY OF INFUSED FOODS

Let's start by saying that the only thing you can count on when calculating potency is that you'll get it wrong. This by no means is intended to doubt your math skills. It is just a fact we all must embrace. Unless you have a lab and are willing to spend some serious dollars (and even then...), the best you can do is make a good approximation of the THC level in your edibles.

Why is that? Well, determining potency simply involves too many unknowns: factors like the quality, age, potency, and type of the strain, as well as the quality of the decarboxylation process, are all critical in determining the level of high to be expected. But that's not all—the type and quality of the carrier are also factors. Coconut oil, butter, olive oil, and alcohol absorb THC with different levels of efficacy.

So now that we've established that a potency "window" is what we're aiming for, let's find out how to make the best estimate.

STEP 1

Check the Strain Label

The strain's potency is typically marked on the bag it came in. Make sure you note the level of THC, rather than THCa. Some producers' labels indicate the THCa level, which converts to THC at a ratio of 0.88 (i.e., 100 mg THCa = 88 mg THC).

STEP 2

Figure Out Your Strain's THC Content in mg

A milligram is a thousandth of a gram, so each gram contains 1,000mg. If your strain's THC level is 15 percent, each gram of flower's THC content can be calculated as follows: 1,000 mg x 15% = 150 mg THC.

STEP 3

Figure Out Your Recipe's THC Content in mg

Let's say you are using 1 ounce of marijuana (28 g) to make cannabutter. Multiply that number of grams by the level of THC per gram in your strain, as follows: 28 x 150 mg = 4,200 mg THC.

STEP 4

Figure Out Your Recipe's THC Content Per
Serving in mg

The recipe you're making, the one that contains 4,200
mg THC, will yield 3 cups of cannabutter.

All that's left to do is divide the total potency of THC
by the total number of servings. To determine the
amount of THC in 1 cup of cannabutter, divide the
total dosage by three: 4,200 mg ÷ 3 = 1,400 mg THC.
If you use the 1 cup of cannabutter to make
40 cookies, then each cookie contains 1,400 mg ÷ 40
= 35 mg THC.

STEP 5

Apply a Discount

Now we step away from the science and move on to
the art. It's impossible to know how much potency
is lost during the decarboxylation and cooking
processes and as a result of the combination with
the carrier. But you can be certain that not all
of the THC is retained during the cooking process.
The best choice: figure things out through a lot of
trial and error. Eventually, after several attempts,
you'll be able to get a sense of where you're at.
I apply a conservative 20 percent discount, but that
may be lower or higher in your experience by a fair
margin. After you apply a 20 percent discount, your
35 mg of THC per cookie translates to 35 mg x 0.8 =
28 mg THC.

The trick to enriching any dish with the beneficial attributes of marijuana is in taking one of the ingredients—typically the fat (butter or oil)—through an infusion process. This is a lengthy process that takes anywhere from 6 hours to months, but the reward for doing it right is guaranteed. Therefore, to allow space for culinary spontaneity, I advise making large batches of infused ingredients at a time, as they easily last for months or longer.

For you mavericks out there who find following instructions to the letter somewhat challenging (yours truly included), I recommend that you find your stickler alter ego and carry out these recipes in the most precise manner possible. Variations to either the decarboxylation process (see p. 22) or the infusion may result in a sub-optimal extraction of the plant's psychoactive properties. In other words, it may screw up the potency.

01.
Infusions

Advanced   *6h*   *Vegetarian*

CANNABUTTER

*The most common means to introduce THC into edibles is cannabutter.
It preserves the THC's magic and beautifully integrates it into a dish. I
recommend making a large batch, as the process is slow, and I've yet to find
myself throwing away cannabutter (you'll find good use for it). Cook with
it, bake with it, add it to pastas, or drizzle it on popcorn—whatever you do,
you're sure to enjoy.*

½ oz (14 g) good-quality strain, finely
   crushed and decarboxylated (see p. 22)
1 cup unsalted butter

1 cup water
Cheesecloth

1|

In a pot over low heat, combine the butter and water. Simmer until the butter melts completely (the water prevents the butter from burning).

2|

Once the butter has fully melted, add the ground, decarboxylated cannabis and stir gently. Cover and simmer, stirring every 30 minutes for 6 hours (check periodically to make sure the butter doesn't reach a boil). Remove from the heat and set aside to cool for 5 minutes.

3|

Line a sieve with cheesecloth and place it over a glass bowl. Strain the butter into the bowl, pushing down on the mixture with the back of a spoon in order to squeeze out every drop of the butter. Discard the contents of the cheesecloth.

4|

Cover the mixture and place it in the refrigerator for at least 1 hour so it can harden. The butter will separate from the water; using a fork or a spatula, remove the butter and discard the water.

5|

Transfer the butter to a well-marked storage dish and keep it in the fridge for several weeks or in the freezer for up to 6 months.

Potency: If you're using a 15% THC strain this recipe yields approximately 1680 mg of THC. See how to calculate potency on page 24.

*An Important Note Regarding Cannabutter
When you use cannabutter, always slice it vertically. Each cannabinoid has a different molecular weight, and gravity plays a role here. The butter that sinks to the bottom of the batch will have slightly different qualities than that at the top.*

Advanced   12h   Vegan

CANNABIS OIL

Cannabis-infused oils are great for cooking, baking, sautéing, frying, and even making salad dressing. On occasion I'll even put a small bowl of infused olive oil and aged balsamic vinegar for friends to dip bread into. Whatever you're using it for, make a big batch. The process is long, and the infused oil can be used for months. The two most common oils to infuse are olive and canola. That said, you can use the exact same recipe with any other kind of oil.

10 g cannabis, finely crushed and decarboxylated
  (see p. 22)
1 cup extra-virgin olive oil
Cheesecloth

1|

In a double boiler over very low heat, combine the oil
and the crushed, decarboxylated cannabis. Cook for
6 hours, stirring every 30 minutes or so.* Cooking in
water allows for gentler cooking, which is important,
as too much heat or an uneven distribution of heat
will harm the potency of oil. Once the cooking is
done, remove from the heat and let the oil
sit overnight.

2|

Place the cheesecloth over a sieve, place the sieve
over a bowl, and strain the oil.** Press down on the
plant matter with the back of a spoon to squeeze out
every drop of the oil into the bowl.

3|

Sterilize a glass jar with an airtight lid by washing it
with soap and hot water and filling it with boiling
water. Let the boiling water sit for 5 minutes and
then discard the water. Allow it to air-dry.

4|

Pour the infused oil into the glass jar. Close the
container with the airtight lid and store in a cool,
dark place. If you keep it clean and cool, it should keep
for up to a year.

* Make sure the oil never reaches its boiling point.
** Gently press.

Potency: **If you're using a 15% THC strain, this recipe
yields approximately 1,200 mg of THC. See how to
calculate potency on p. 24.**

Advanced   8h   Vegan

CANNABIS-INFUSED COCONUT OIL

Coconut oil is arguably the best fat to infuse with cannabinoids due its high saturated fat content. In addition, coconut oil is a healthier fat than canola and butter, as it boasts a fairly wide list of potential health benefits. Since infused coconut oil remains solid at room temperature, it's also widely used for topicals and to fill gelatin capsules.

2 cups high-quality coconut oil
Cheesecloth

½ oz (14 g) good-quality strain, finely crushed and decarboxylated (see p. 22)

1|

Place the coconut oil in a double boiler over low heat and cook for a few minutes. Once the coconut oil has melted, add the strain and mix gently but thoroughly (there's no need to cover).

2|

Simmer uncovered for 6 to 8 hours, making sure you're using the minimal amount of heat possible and that the oil never shows signs of reaching its boiling point (a bubble here and there is fine). Stir gently every hour or so. Remove from the heat.

3|

Place a sieve over a bowl and line it with a double-layered cheesecloth. Pour the coconut oil and plant matter into the sieve and let it drip into the bowl for 15 minutes. Using the back of a tablespoon, gently press down on the plant matter to ensure every drop of oil squeezes through the filter. You can compost the cannabis, as it no longer has THC in it.

4|

Sterilize a glass jar with an airtight lid by washing it with soap and hot water and filling it with boiling water. Let the boiling water sit for 5 minutes and then discard the water. Set aside to air-dry.

5|

Pour the infused coconut oil into the glass jar and set aside to cool to room temperature (it should take roughly 1 hour). Make sure you leave the jar uncovered to prevent condensation. Close the container with the airtight lid and store in a cool, dark place. If you keep it clean and cool, it should keep for months.

Potency: If you're using a 15% THC strain, this recipe yields approximately 1,680 mg of THC. See how to calculate potency on p. 24.

Advanced   20min   Vegetarian

CANNA MAYO

If you're still buying store-bought mayonnaise, I suggest exploring the homemade version. Making mayo at home is super-quick and super-easy, and it offers twice the taste. Mayonnaise is a great carrier for savory edibles. Use this cannabis-infused version to spike up your hamburgers, spinach dips, or salad dressings.

1 large egg at room temperature

1 tbsp Dijon mustard, plus more as needed

1 tbsp white wine vinegar

1 tsp freshly squeezed lemon juice

¼ tsp salt, plus more as needed

¼ tsp white pepper, plus more as needed

Pinch cayenne pepper (optional)

1 cup cannabis-infused oil (canola based; see p. 30),
   plus more as needed

Water if needed

You can use a food processor for this recipe.
If you choose to do so, make sure you use a small bowl
or double the recipe, as the mayonnaise requires ample
contact with the blade. Another good alternative is
to use a hand emulsifier or an electric whisk, as these
allow for better texture control.

1|

In a mixing bowl or in the bowl of a food processor fitted with the "S" blade, combine the egg, the mustard, the vinegar, the lemon juice, the ¼ tsp salt, the ¼ tsp white pepper, and the pinch of cayenne pepper, if using. Whisk or process for 1 whole minute, or until the ingredients reach an even, foamy consistency.

2|

While whisking or processing constantly, slowly add the 1 cup cannabis-infused oil in tiny drops. Doing this slowly and patiently is critical to allow for proper emulsification.

3|

When all the oil has been added, use a spatula to scrape the bottom and edges of the bowl. Whisk or process again for another 10 to 20 seconds to ensure the mixture is fully blended.

4|

Taste and adjust the seasoning if need be. If the mayonnaise is too thin, you can add a bit more oil, or if it is too thick, you can add a few drops of water. If the mayonnaise mixture "breaks," or fails to hold together, add a bit more mustard and whisk again.

5|

Store in an airtight and sterilized glass container in the fridge. The mayonnaise should keep until the expiration date of the egg is reached.

Potency: If you're using a 15% THC strain, this recipe yields approximately 1,200 mg of THC. See how to calculate potency on p. 24.

Advanced   *1w-6m*   *Vegan*

WEED TINCTURES: WHAT YOU NEED TO KNOW

Tinctures are alcohol-based extracts. Like oil and butter, alcohol is a great carrier for THC. Tinctures are a great low-calorie alternative to traditional edibles. Many people take tinctures sublingually rather than by swallowing them, as it speeds up the effect. Since it is much easier to control the dosage of a tincture, it's a better alternative to edibles for those who are looking for a small dose that won't interrupt their day.

Tinctures last for years when stored in a cool and dark place, which means you can make large quantities of them. This is also a good piece of advice, as tinctures can be extremely concentrated (hence, very potent). Once you prepare a batch, test it carefully—take 1 drop and wait to see the effect and slowly increase the dose till you reach the desired result.

The "industry" standard for the best type of solvent is Everclear, a brand name of pure grain alcohol (PGA), due to its high alcohol content. The higher the percentage of alcohol, the greater the THC extraction from the plant matter will be. But any alcohol that is 40% proof and up will have good levels of extraction. Just remember to use gloves when handling tinctures, as they can seep into skin pores and lead to unintended medication.

1 oz (28 g) cannabis, finely crushed and decarboxylated
  (see p. 22)
2 Mason jars

High-proof alcohol (Everclear is best), to cover
Cheesecloth
2 coffee filters

1|

Pour the crushed, decarboxylated plant matter into
one of the Mason jars. Add just enough of the alcohol
to completely immerse the flower—no more—and
mix together.

2|

Close the jar and set aside in a cool, dark place for
one week to six months: the longer, the better THC
extraction. Shaking it once every couple of days helps
the cannabinoids absorb.

3|

Using a double layer of the cheesecloth, filter the
tincture into a separate Mason jar. As you filter the
tincture, press down gently on the plant matter to
make sure every drop of THC gets saved for later use.
Repeat the process, this time using the coffee filters
instead of the cheesecloth, transferring back into the
original jar, yielding a clear liquid.

4|

Transfer the tincture to an opaque dropper bottle and
use as needed. Store in a cool, dark place.

Potency: *If you're using a 15% THC strain, this recipe
yields approximately 3,360 mg of THC, which is
extremely potent. Consume responsibly. See how to
calculate potency on p. 24.*

Advanced   *32h*   *Vegetarian*

MARIJUANA-INFUSED HONEY

This is my favorite infusion: ingredients that have great healing properties working together to create the first ganja superfood. Use it on bread, in tea, in salad vinaigrettes, or just by the spoonful. However you use it, this recipe tends to be potent, so start slow. The coconut oil is added to make sure the THC is fully absorbed into the honey, and its effect on the taste is marginal.

18 oz (500 g) high-quality honey
10 g cannabis, crushed and decarboxylated (see p. 22)
2 tbsp coconut oil

Cheesecloth
Kitchen twine

1|

Fold the cheesecloth into a double layer. Place the decarboxylated cannabis in its center and roll it up, creating a small pouch with the cannabis at its center. Using kitchen twine, tie it securely so the cannabis cannot seep out of the cheesecloth while cooking; make sure it's not too tightly wrapped, as you want the honey to sift through the cloth.

2|

Place the honey, the coconut oil, and the cheesecloth-wrapped cannabis in a heavy pot over very low heat. The cheesecloth will float, but don't worry about it— it will still do the work.

3|

Cook for 8 hours, stirring every hour or so to allow the cannabis to fully interact with the honey (it's very important to make sure the heat is on the very lowest setting; if the honey reaches a boil its taste and properties will suffer). Remove from the heat and set aside at room temperature for 24 hours.

4|

Heat the honey up a bit to liquify it, and remove the cheesecloth pouch. Using your hands or tongs, squeeze whatever you can out of the pouch and discard it. Transfer the honey to a sterilized can or jar; it will keep for months. If the honey gets too stiff, you can always warm it up a bit.

Potency: If you're using a 15% THC strain, this recipe yields approximately 1,200 mg of THC. See how to calculate potency on p. 24.

Simple   7-10 days   Vegan

CANNAVODKA

Cannabis-infused alcohol is a way to enjoy the effects of two catalysts together. Mixing the two intoxicants, or "cross-fading," does come with some risk. There's not much research on the phenomenon, so we're left to use our own observation to determine its risks and benefits. I find that different people react very differently to cross-fading: some argue that it amplifies the effect (hence, it makes you much higher and drunker), and some say it decreases your energy levels and makes you wasted very quickly. However you feel about this fusion, I'd advise to tread carefully until you feel comfortable with the right dosage.

The below recipe, just to be clear, is not a tincture. It is less concentrated and meant to be used as an ingredient in place of an alcoholic beverage or as a standalone drink. If you'd like to prepare a tincture for general use, see p. 36.

10 g cannabis, crushed and decarboxylated (see p. 22)
1 Mason jar
1 (750 ml) bottle your favorite vodka (40% proof & up)
Cheesecloth

1|

Pour the crushed, decarboxylated plant matter into the Mason jar. Add the entire bottle of vodka (reserve the bottle).

2|

Close the jar and set aside in a cool, dark place for 7 to 10 days: the longer, the better THC extraction. Shake it once every day to help the cannabinoids absorb.

3|

Using a double layer of the cheesecloth and a wide funnel, filter the vodka back into the original bottle. As you filter the vodka, press the cheesecloth tight to extract as much of the THC as you can.

4|

Store in a cool, dark place.

Potency: If you're using a 15% THC strain, this recipe yields approximately 1,200 mg of THC. See how to calculate potency on p. 24.

Happy Energy Bars -45-

Double-Intoxicated Jell-O Shots -47-

Mango-Strawberry-Coconut Potsicles -48-

The Best Pot Brownies You've Ever Tasted! -51-

The Mile-High Dates 'n' Nuts Sausage -54-

Grandma Pecan Bars with Extra Zing -56-

High Fudge Sundae -59-

Happy Biscotti -60-

Chirpy Fruit Dipped in Chocolate -64-

Hazelbud & Chocolate Spread -65-

Tahini and Honey Weedoockies -67-

Cake Pot-Pops -69-

Chocolate-Chip Cookie Dough in a Skillet: A Version for
Every Mood -73-

Baked (Give Me) S'mores Cups -77-

The taste that's most closely associated with edibles is sweet. Sweets have long been the taste of choice signifying love and happiness; it's no wonder, I guess, that we tend to focus more on them when we're feeling the love.

The people in our gang are categorized as being members of either Camp Pretzel (the savories) or Camp Oreo (the sweets). I'm a proud member of Camp Pretzel myself, but I'm the first to admit that sweet canna-recipes are often preferable to their savory counterparts due to their ability to better disguise the aftertaste of the weed. And as I'm married to a passionate member of Camp Oreo who prefers sweet dishes over anything, I take pleasure in the encouraging support I receive for exploring the fascinating world of sweet canna-dishes.

Each of the recipes in this chapter have been designed, tried, and tested by yours truly and my neighboring culinary community. It wasn't easy, but we pushed through and eventually managed to present an amazing array of recipes. Do enjoy!

02.
Sweet High of Mine

Moderate *3h* *Vegetarian*

HAPPY ENERGY BARS

If you're like me and you're into meditative hikes, this is the perfect energy bar. It gives you both the kick you need to climb each hill and the serenity to appreciate being in the moment.

 12

2½ cups old-fashioned rolled oats

1 tbsp vegetable oil

½ cup chopped pecans

2 tbsp white sesame seeds

2 tbsp sunflower seeds

⅓ cup light brown sugar

¼ cup cannabutter (see p. 28)

¼ cup honey

3 tbsp maple syrup

1 tsp vanilla extract

Pinch salt

1 tsp ground cinnamon (optional)

½ cup chopped dried dates

¼ cup dark chocolate chips

1|

Preheat the oven to 350°F. Line a 9-inch square baking dish with parchment paper and coat it with the oil.

2|

Place the oats, pecans, sesame and sunflower seeds in the oiled dish and bake for 8 to 10 minutes, or until they brown lightly. Remove from the oven and transfer to a mixing bowl. Set aside.

3|

In a pan over medium heat, combine the brown sugar, cannabutter, honey, and maple syrup and cook, mixing lightly, for 5 minutes. Remove from the heat and add the vanilla and salt and the cinnamon, if using.

4|

After the two mixtures have cooled for 10 minutes, combine them and stir in the remaining ingredients.

5|

Evenly spread the mix into the lined baking dish and, using the bottom part of a cup, press it down gently until it has the condensed consistency of an energy bar. Cover and let sit in the fridge for at least 2 hours.

6|

Remove from the baking dish and, using a wet, sharp chef's knife, slice into 12 pieces. Wrap each piece individually with parchment paper and store for up to 1 month in a cool, dry place or in the fridge. Happy travels!

Potency: If you're using a 15% THC strain, this recipe yields approximately 35 mg of THC per serving. See how to calculate potency on p. 24.

Simple   *40min*   *Vegetarian**

DOUBLE-INTOXICATED JELL-O SHOTS

For those of you who like the double kick that marijuana and alcohol provide, this is a great, cute little starter for a night of laughs and deep conversations. It's a particularly great outcome considering the truly minimal amount of work required. I'll drink to that!

 12

1 (3 oz) package Jell-O gelatin of your choice
   (I recommend using pineapple or watermelon)
1 cup boiling water
½ cup ice-cold water

½ cup cannavodka (see p. 40)
2 tbsp freshly grated lime zest
¼ cup fresh pineapple, cut into 12 small pieces, or
   gummy bears (optional but recommended)

1|

Empty the Jell-O powder into a heat-resistant mixing bowl and add the boiling water. Stir continuously for 2 minutes, or until the powder is completely dissolved.

2|

Add the cold water and cannavodka and stir for 1 additional minute, or until all the ingredients have integrated.

3|

Pour into shot glasses. Sprinkle the lime zest on top of the shots and, if you choose, dunk a pineapple slice or gummy bear in each one. I also recommend placing a small spoon or cut straw in the glass to help dislodge the Jell-O shot once it's stabilized.

4|

Place in the fridge for at least 30 minutes and for up to 1 week.

5|

Serve.

Potency: *If you're using a 15% THC strain, this recipe yields approximately 13 mg of THC per serving. See how to calculate potency on p. 24.*

*Contains gelatin.

Simple   *6h*   *Vegan*

MANGO-STRAWBERRY-COCONUT POTSICLES

The secret to great popsicles… well, there is none. It is virtually impossible to get this recipe wrong. On a hot summer afternoon, these potsicles are a perfect match that ensures both a refreshing delight and giddy conversation.

 8

3 cups cubed mango

2 cups unsweetened coconut milk
 (use vanilla-flavored if you prefer that zing)

3 tbsp freshly squeezed orange juice

2 tbsp marijuana-infused honey (see p. 39)

1 cup stemmed and thinly sliced fresh strawberries

10 popsicle molds

1|

In the jug of a blender, combine the mango, coconut milk, orange juice, and marijuana-infused honey and puree until smooth.

2|

Evenly divide the strawberry slices among the popsicle molds.

3|

Fill each mold with the mango puree. Tap gently on each mold to make sure the liquid fills in between the strawberry slices.

4|

Freeze for at least 6 hours or overnight.

5|

Serve.

Potency: If you're using a 15% THC strain, this recipe yields approximately 12 mg of THC per serving. See how to calculate potency on p. 24.

Moderate   *45min*   *Vegetarian*

THE BEST POT BROWNIES YOU'VE EVER TASTED!

No self-respecting cannabis cookbook is complete without a recipe for pot brownies. Brownies have become almost synonymous with edibles. There are as many recipes for pot brownies as there are for brownies. This recipe isn't the simplest and quickest one, but it will give you the ultimate indulgence of gluttonous sin!

 20

10½ oz (300 g) dark chocolate (70% cocoa and up)

½ cup cannabutter (see p. 28)

½ cup + 1 tbsp unsalted butter, plus more for greasing

1½ cups confectioners' sugar

5 whole large eggs

2 tsp high-quality vanilla extract

2 cups all-purpose flour

1 hearty tsp baking powder

3½ oz (100 g) white chocolate

¾ cup whole hazelnuts (optional)

1|

Preheat the oven to 340°F.

2|

Combine the dark chocolate, the ½ cup + 1 tbsp butter, and the cannabutter in a pan and place it over a pot of gently simmering water. Stir until the chocolate and butters are fully melted together. Remove from the heat and set aside to cool down a bit.

3|

Using an electric mixer, beat together the confectioners' sugar, eggs, and vanilla extract until you get a solid fluff. Once the chocolate mixture has cooled down a bit (otherwise it will start cooking the eggs), slowly add it to the egg mixture, mixing on low speed until it is fully integrated.

4|

Add the flour and baking powder and continue to slowly mix until you reach an even consistency—but no more than necessary.

5|

Using the butter, grease a 9-inch x 13-inch baking dish and pour in the brownie batter. Spread it evenly in the dish.

6|

Break up the white chocolate into small pieces and insert them evenly into the brownie batter. Press gently with your fingers so the pieces completely absorb into the batter. If you choose to add them, gently press in the hazelnuts so they're half in and half out of the batter.

7|

Bake for 30 to 35 minutes, or until the center of the brownies are moist but not runny. Insert a toothpick to test the doneness; only chocolate should cover it, not batter. Remove from the oven and set aside to cool.

Potency: If you're using a 15% THC strain, this recipe yields approximately 40 mg of THC per serving. See how to calculate potency on p. 24.

Moderate   1h/90min   Vegan

THE MILE-HIGH DATES 'N' NUTS SAUSAGE

This gluten-free, lactose-free, and bake-free vegan treat will take just a few minutes of your time. Keep it in a sealed container for up to 2 weeks for when things are hectic and you want a small dose of patience.

20

1 cup peeled and broken pecans

1 cup peeled and broken pistachios

½ cup peeled and broken walnuts

Dash ground cinnamon (optional)

¼ cup light brown sugar

3 tbsp marijuana-infused honey (see p. 39)

15 dried dates, seeded and finely chopped

¼ cup shredded coconut

1|

In a mixing bowl, combine all the nuts and, if you'd like, the cinnamon. Set aside.

2|

In a small pot over low heat, combine the brown sugar and honey and cook, making sure it does not boil and stirring constantly, until the mixture reaches an even consistency.

Add the chopped dates and cook, stirring constantly, for 5 minutes, or until the dates become very soft and almost liquify. Remove from the heat.

3|

Stir in the nut mixture thoroughly, until everything is completely integrated. Place the mixture in the fridge for at least 30 minutes (1 hour is better).

4|

Create two sausage-like cylinders. Make sure they are as tight as you can make them. Spread the coconut flakes on a flat plate and roll the cylinders around in them until they are thoroughly covered.

5|

Wrap the cylinders as tightly as you can in plastic wrap and store in the freezer for 30 minutes.

6|

Slice each sausage into about 10 to 12 discs and serve.

Potency: If you're using a 15% THC strain, this recipe yields approximately 7 mg of THC per serving. See how to calculate potency on p. 24.

Moderate   1h   Vegetarian

GRANDMA PECAN BARS WITH EXTRA ZING

As a youngster (too many years ago), the dessert I yearned for most of all was my grandma's pecan bars. The juicy, sweet, and nutty taste of them raised the bar (bar... get it?) for all other sweet dishes in my life. I hope she'd be proud of the fact that I've taken some creative steps and transitioned this recipe so it not only lifts the bar (yes... again) on a culinary level but also in a more spiritual sense.

24

For the crust:

2½ cups all-purpose flour, plus more for dusting

2 sticks unsalted butter, softened

⅔ cup confectioners' sugar

½ teaspoon salt

For the filling:

1½ cups light brown sugar, packed

5 tbsp cannabutter (see p. 28)

3 tbsp unsalted butter

½ cup honey

2 tbsp heavy cream

1 lb pecans, coarsely chopped

1|

Preheat the oven to 350°F.

2|

Make the crust: Combine all the crust ingredients in the bowl of a food processor fitted with the "S" blade and process on low until it forms a crumbly mix—but (and this is important!) stop before the mixture comes together into a dough.

3|

Line a 9-inch x 13-inch baking dish with parchment paper and scatter the dough crumbs on top of it. Place another sheet of parchment paper on top of it and press down firmly and evenly with your fingers. Remove the upper parchment paper and bake for 20 minutes, or until the edges become golden brown. Remove from the oven.

4|

Make the filling: While the crust is getting crusty, combine all the filling ingredients except the pecans in a saucepan over medium heat. Cook, stirring constantly, for a good 5 minutes, or until the mixture liquifies. Then, reduce the heat and simmer for 1 minute more to let it thicken a bit. Stir in the pecans and remove from the heat.

5|

Don't let the crust cool: immediately after you take it out of the oven, pour the topping into the crust and spread it evenly using a spatula or a tablespoon. Return to the oven for 20 minutes. Remove from the oven and set aside to cool for 15 minutes.

6|

Slice into squares and serve.

Potency: If you're using a 15% THC strain, this recipe yields approximately 21 mg of THC per serving. See how to calculate potency on p. 24.

Simple   20min   Vegetarian

HIGH FUDGE SUNDAE

When you're preparing a hot fudge sundae, I say go all out. This isn't the time to be focused on nutrition or to be health conscious. Today we eat… we'll run another lap tomorrow. The golden rule is that whatever makes you smile should go in it. Personally, I'm a devout follower of this rule, so I've taken the liberty to make some sinful choices below.

 4

1¾ cup heavy cream

½ cup packed light brown sugar

⅓ cup light corn syrup or honey

3 tbsp high-fat (at least 22%) cocoa powder (not Dutch process)

¼ tsp salt

7 oz (200 g) finely chopped bittersweet chocolate

1 tbsp unsalted butter

1 tbsp cannabutter (see p. 28)

2 tbsp confectioners' sugar

1 tsp vanilla extract

8 scoops of the best-tasting vanilla ice cream you can get your hands on

8 fresh cherries, pitted

Crushed pecans, chopped pistachios, Oreo bits, and fresh-cut banana slices, for topping

1|

Place a stainless-steel mixing bowl in the freezer for 20 minutes.

2|

In a saucepan over low heat, combine ¾ cup of the cream with the brown sugar, corn syrup, cocoa powder, and salt. Bring to a simmer and cook, whisking constantly, for about 5 minutes, or until the sugar dissolves and the mixture thickens.

3|

Stir in the chocolate, butter, and cannabutter and continue cooking until the chocolate melts. Remove from the heat and set aside to cool.

4|

Add the remaining 1 cup of the cream to the cold mixing bowl and whip on medium-high speed for 3 minutes. After the whipped cream's volume grows, add the confectioners' sugar and vanilla extract and mix on high until the whipped cream has reached a solid consistency. Make sure not to over-whip, as it may break down.

5|

Now for the assembly: pour a little of the hot fudge sauce into the bottoms of each serving cup. Add equal portions of the ice cream and plenty of the toppings to each serving and then really give it a boost of the hot fudge sauce. Cover it all with some fresh whipped cream and then add some more whipped cream for good karma. Don't forget the cherry on top!

Potency: If you're using a 15% THC strain and assuming you use all the chocolate syrup, this recipe yields approximately 13 mg of THC per serving. See how to calculate potency on p. 24.

Simple   1h   Vegetarian

HAPPY BISCOTTI

These classic Italian biscuits are super crunchy and great for dipping in coffee or wine. My friends just love to reach over the fridge for the cookie jar filled with these tasty mood enhancers. If you are in a truly adventurous mode, dip it in chocolate that's been melted together with more cannabutter.

30

¾ cup confectioners' sugar

¼ cup cannabutter (see p. 28)

3 whole large eggs

1 large egg white, lightly beaten

1 tsp vanilla extract

3 cups all-purpose flour

1 tsp baking powder

¾ cup chocolate chips

½ cup dried cranberries

½ cup chopped hazelnuts or pistachios

2 tsp instant espresso powder

2 tsp freshly grated orange zest

1|

Preheat the oven to 350°F. Line a baking sheet with parchment paper.

2|

Using an electric mixer, cream together the confectioners' sugar and cannabutter until you get a fluffy, even texture. Beat in the eggs, the egg white, and the vanilla on low speed until they fully blend in.

3|

In a separate mixing bowl, sift together the flour and baking powder. Gradually integrate the dry ingredients into the liquid mixture. Stir in the chocolate chips, cranberries, hazelnuts, espresso, and orange zest and knead thoroughly until a dough forms.

4|

Shape the dough into 2 cylinders, each roughly 1 foot long. Place each log on the baking sheet and flatten each out to about 1 ½ inches thick.

5|

Bake for about 35 minutes, or until the edges are golden. Check the center; it should be hard when pressed on with your finger. Remove from the oven and set aside to cool on a rack.

6|

When the loaves are cool enough, slice them diagonally into ¼-inch-thick slices.

7|

Return the slices to the baking sheet, flat side facing up. Bake for another 15 minutes, or until they start turning light brown. Remove from the oven. After the biscotti have cooled completely, store in an airtight container for up to 1 month.

Potency: If you're using a 15% THC strain, this recipe yields approximately 14 mg of THC per serving. See how to calculate potency on p. 24.

Simple   30min   Vegan

CHIRPY FRUIT DIPPED IN CHOCOLATE

This simple, quick, and blissful hors d'oeuvre is guaranteed to liven up any social occasion or romantic getaway. I highly recommend adding one (or more) of the toppings, as they disguise the canna taste and add a well-received crunch. Feel free to play around with different fruits, as canna-chocolate dip really has no favorites. Also, don't throw away the remaining chocolate dip; keep it in the fridge and then warm it up for another use—either for dipping or to drizzle over ice cream or cakes. Enjoy!

 8-10

10 good-looking fresh strawberries

2 fresh nectarines, cored and cut into large wedges

2 green apples, stemmed and cut into large wedges

½ pineapple, peeled and cut into large triangles

2½ cups dark chocolate chips

3 tbsp cannabis-infused coconut oil (see p. 33)

Dried coconut, chopped almond pieces, chopped sweetened pecans, for topping (optional but recommended)

1|

Line a baking sheet with parchment paper.

2|

Combine the chocolate chips and the cannabis-infused coconut oil in a microwave-safe bowl. Zap it on high in 20-second intervals, stirring well in between each interval, until the chocolate has completely melted and is smooth and consistent. Set aside to rest until the chocolate has cooled down a bit.

3|

Dip each piece of fruit in the melted chocolate, count to five, and then dip again (let's be sinful).

4|

Roll the chocolate-dipped section of the fruit in your desired topping and place it on the prepared baking sheet. Set aside at room temperature for at least 20 minutes (if you will not be consuming it right away, put it in the fridge).

5|

Serve.

Potency: If you're using a 15% THC strain, and assuming you use all the chocolate syrup, this recipe yields approximately 15-19 mg of THC per serving. See how to calculate potency on p. 24.

Simple   *20min*   *Vegan*

HAZELBUD AND CHOCOLATE SPREAD

The union of roasted hazelnuts and chocolate is extremely addictive, so pace yourself. This Nutella-like (but much better) spread is a perfect tasty snack that will keep you at cruising altitude throughout the day. I use it in sandwiches and Saturday-morning crepes.

 20

1 cup hazelnuts, preferably peeled

¼ cup confectioners' sugar

3 tbsp cannabis-infused coconut oil (see p. 33)

1 tbsp hazelnut or canola oil

1 tbsp unsweetened cocoa powder

½ tsp vanilla extract

½ tsp salt

12 oz dark chocolate chips

1|

Preheat the oven to 350°F. Line a baking sheet with parchment paper.

2|

Spread the hazelnuts in a single layer on the prepared baking sheet and toast them for 15 minutes. Remove from the oven. If they had skin on them, now is the time to rub them gently with a towel to remove whatever skin you can.

3|

In the jug of a powerful blender (preferable) or the bowl of a food processor fitted with the "S" blade, grind the roasted hazelnuts into a fine powder. Add the confectioners' sugar, cannabis-infused coconut oil, hazelnut oil, cocoa powder, vanilla, and salt and continue processing until the mixture is smooth and even.

4|

Place the chocolate chips in a microwave-safe bowl. Zap it on high in 30-second intervals, stirring well in between each interval, until the chocolate has completely melted and is smooth and consistent.

5|

Add the chocolate to the hazelnut mixture in the blender or food processor and pulse until just combined. (Pulse it as little as possible; the more you pulse, the firmer the spread will be after it cools.)

6|

Transfer to a sterilized jar and keep in the fridge for up to 3 weeks.

Potency: If you're using a 15% THC strain this recipe yields approximately 8 mg of THC per serving (a serving represents a thin layer of spread on a standard bread slice). See how to calculate potency on p. 24.

Moderate   *2/3h*   *Vegetarian*

TAHINI AND HONEY WEEDOOCKIES

A great recipe for sweet-toothers and health conscious cooks.

 15

¼ cup cannabutter, softened (see p. 28)

¼ cup superfine sugar

3 tbsp unsalted butter

3 hearty tbsp honey

1¼ cups self-rising flour

¼ cup + 1 tbsp raw tahini

¼ cup crushed pecans

Freshly grated zest of 1 lemon

1 tsp ground cinnamon

½ cup confectioners' sugar, for dusting

1|

Preheat the oven to 350°F. Line a baking sheet with parchment paper.

2|

In a mixing bowl, using an electric mixer on medium speed, beat together the cannabutter, sugar, butter, and honey until the mixture reaches an even consistency.

3|

Add the flour, tahini, pecans, lemon zest, and cinnamon. Reduce the speed to low and mix until everything is well combined. Cover the bowl with a towel and place in the fridge for at least 1 hour.

4|

With slightly wet hands, roll the chilled dough into ping-pong ball size balls. Place on the prepared baking sheet and press gently with your finger to flatten the balls. Generously dust the confectioners' sugar on top of the cookies.

5|

Bake for 10 to 15 minutes. The cookies are ready when their edges start browning. Don't overbake, as they will dry out. Remove from the oven and set aside to cool slightly.

6|

Serve warm.

Potency: *If you're using a 15% THC strain, this recipe yields approximately 28 mg of THC per serving. See how to calculate potency on p. 24.*

Advanced   *3h*   *Vegetarian*

CAKE POT-POPS

A sweet bite-size recipe for the high-entertainer. If you have some leftover 'happy' cake save it for some ice cream mix-ins or to add to a smoothie.

 40

For the cake:

1¾ cups all-purpose flour

½ tsp baking powder

½ tsp salt

¼ tsp baking soda

1 cup confectioners' sugar

½ cup cannabutter, softened (see p. 28)

1 whole large egg

1 tsp vanilla extract

Unsalted butter, for greasing

1 cup whole milk

Few drops green food coloring

For the frosting:

1 cup confectioners' sugar

6 tbsp unsalted butter, softened

¼ cup (1 oz) cream cheese, softened

1 tsp vanilla extract

For the coating:

1 cup semisweet chocolate chips

40 green M&Ms (optional)

40 lollipop sticks

1|

Preheat the oven to 350°F.

2|

Make the cake:

In a mixing bowl, sift together the flour, baking powder, salt, and baking soda.

3|

In a separate mixing bowl, using an electric mixer on medium speed, cream together the confectioners' sugar and cannabutter until they have fully integrated with one another (but no longer). Add the milk, egg, and vanilla extract and beat for another 2 minutes.

4|

Reduce the speed to low and add the food coloring and dry ingredients mixture to the wet mixture. Mix well, making sure there are no lumps or dry patches left.

5|

Grease a 9-inch x 13-inch baking dish with the butter. Pour in the cake batter and spread it evenly. Bake for 35 minutes, or until a toothpick inserted in the center comes out clean. Remove from the oven and allow the cake to cool completely.

6|

Make the frosting: In a mixing bowl, using an electric mixer, combine all the ingredients and mix until well combined.

7|

Using your hands or a fork, crumble the cake into a large mixing bowl. Add ¾ of the frosting to the bowl containing the crumbled cake and, using an electric mixer, mix on low speed. Add more of the frosting by the tablespoon until the mixture reaches your desired texture (it will become increasingly moist as you add frosting).

8|

Remove a tablespoon of the frosting-cake mixture and, using slightly wet hands, roll it into a ping-pong ball size ball.

9|

Line a baking sheet with parchment paper. Place the cake balls on the prepared baking sheet and place in the fridge for 2 hours.

10|

Place the chocolate chips in a microwave-safe bowl. Zap it on high in 30-second intervals, stirring well in between each interval, until the chocolate has completely melted and is smooth and consistent.

11|

Remove a few cake balls from the fridge at a time. Insert a lollipop stick into each and dunk them into the melted chocolate. If you'd like, add a green M&M to each to mark it as a "special" cake pop. Repeat until all the pops have been dunked.

12|

Return to the fridge until you're ready to eat.

Potency: *If you're using a 15% THC strain, this recipe yields approximately 21 mg of THC per serving. See how to calculate potency on p. 24.*

Moderate   *25min*   *Vegetarian*

CHOCOLATE-CHIP COOKIE DOUGH IN A SKILLET: A VERSION FOR EVERY MOOD

Very few things in life work together better than a sweet munchie craving and this chocolate chip bliss. The childlike looks of anticipation created by the caressing scent of baked chocolate are well worth the work.

 8-10

3 tbsp cannabutter (see recipe on page 28)

4 tbsp unsalted butter, softened, plus more
  for greasing

½ cup packed light brown sugar

⅓ cup granulated sugar

1 cup all-purpose flour

1 cup chocolate chips

1 whole large egg

1 tsp vanilla extract

½ tsp baking soda

Dash salt

½ cup broken pecans (optional)

1|

Preheat the oven to 350°F.

2|

In a large bowl, stir together the cannabutter, 4 tbsp of butter and the sugars. If you're using a hand or stand mixer, use the lowest speed to blend them.

3|

Gradually add in the remaining ingredients, including the pecans, if using, and continue to mix slowly until you reach an even consistency.

4|

Grease a 10-inch cast-iron skillet with the butter. Transfer the batter to the skillet and, using your hands, gently press it down and spread it around.

5|

Bake for 15 to 20 minutes, or until the cookie turns golden brown (if you like your cookies chewy, go for 15 minutes). Remove from the oven and set aside to cool for 5 minutes.

6|

Dig in.

MAKE IT NUTTY

You can choose to add the ½ cup of broken pecans listed as optional in the main recipe or use 5 peanut butter cups (or mix and match) to the ingredient list. Split the batter, pouring half into the skillet. Sprinkle your choice of nutty enjoyment over the batter and then cover it with the remaining batter. Bake as directed.

MAKE IT CHILDISH

Add ½ cup M&Ms and ½ cup gummy bears to the ingredient list. Add them to the batter in step 3, along with the chocolate chips. After you take the skillet out of the oven, add some decorative cake sprinkles and dig in.

MAKE IT SINFUL

Add 5 crushed Oreo cookies and another ½ cup chocolate chips to the batter in step 3. Once it's done, serve with a pint of vanilla bean ice cream, some hot chocolate syrup, and some Schlag (see p. 236).

MAKE IT SPICY AND WEIRD

This one's the outcome of a friendly cooking competition (that I won...). Add 1 tbsp crushed chili flakes and ¼ cup extra-crunchy bacon bits to the batter in step 3, along with the chocolate chips. After you take the skillet out of the oven, sprinkle ½ tsp sea salt over the top and serve. You'll be surprised by how good it is.

Potency: If you're using a 15% THC strain, this recipe yields approximately 30 mg-40 mg of THC per serving. See how to calculate potency on p. 24.

Moderate   *20min*   *Vegetarian**

BAKED (GIVE ME) S'MORES CUPS

This version of the traditional campfire treat doesn't require any handling of fire (always a sensible thing to avoid when soaring high on weed), but it still preserves that sinful, gooey, sugar-bomb feel.

 12-18

1 cup graham cracker crumbs (about 10 graham crackers)

¼ cup confectioners' sugar

3 tbsp cannabutter, at room temperature (see recipe on page 28)

3 tbsp unsalted butter, at room temperature

7 oz (200 g) semisweet chocolate bars, divided into 12 or 18 pieces

6 or 9 large marshmallows, halved

1|

Preheat the oven to 350°F.

2|

In a large bowl, combine the graham cracker crumbs, the sugar, and the cannabutter and mix until it reaches an even consistency. Gradually add in the butter to the mixture, until you're able to roll it into small balls that are not too sandy in texture.

3|

Roll the mixture into 12 or 18 equal-size balls (depending on whether you are using a 12- or 18-hole muffin pan). Press the graham cracker balls into the muffin pan.

4|

Bake for 10 minutes. Promptly remove from the oven (this will allow the crust to bake without burning the gooey filling).

5|

Place 1 piece of chocolate in each cup and top each with a marshmallow half. Return to the oven for an additional 3 to 5 minutes, or until the marshmallows have softened but not melted. Remove from the oven and set aside to cool for 5 to 10 minutes.

6|

Enjoy! If you're into extra-guilty pleasure, you can melt some chocolate in the microwave and drizzle it on top. Either way, prepare yourself for a sugar rush.

Potency: If you're using a 15% THC strain, this recipe yields approximately 17 mg or 26 mg (depending on the muffin pan you're using) of THC per serving. See how to calculate potency on p. 24.

*Contains gelatin.

Salty Abadi-Style Niblets
-80-

Healthy Cannackers (Cannabis Crackers)
-84-

CannaSchug (Spicey Cilantro Chutney)
-85-

Infused Chimichurri Sauce
-87-

Canna-Pesto Mozzarella Swirls
-88-

Crostini with Charred Eggplant and Roasted Canna-Garlic Spread
-90-

Halloumi Cheese, Weed, and Fruit Skewers
-94-

Weed Chai Masala Latte
-97-

Herbal Tea (Literally)
-99-

Magic Smoothies (4 recipes)
-101-

While canna-cooking is a very versatile and new phenomenon, I feel that the "Brownie Effect"—the tendency people have to perceive edibles as being exclusively synonymous with pot brownies and other sweet and intoxicating counterparts—has delayed the creation of, and even a deeper investigation of, savory infused dishes.

However, don't let that confuse you: The realm of "enriched" savory dishes is a world of its own that presents numerous creative alternatives.
In this chapter, I've tried to provide tastes from different genres of cooking-you'll find beverages, finger foods, spreads, and more. Just remember to be cautious with dosage, as we tend to be more indulgent when eating savory foods. An extra bite or two with these can make a big difference in your psychoactive experience.

03.
Savory and Intoxicating

Moderate   45min   Vegetarian

SALTY ABADI-STYLE NIBLETS

Years ago, when I started my first real job, these salty cookies were my daily sin. It got to the point that after my arrival, the office manager had to double the quantity she ordered for the office. What can I say? I'm a sucker for savory dough. When I started creating this book, I knew for sure: These lovely nibbles of salty heaven were going to be transformed into their intoxicating counterparts.

18-21

2 cups all-purpose flour, plus more if needed

½ cup extra-virgin olive oil

¼ cup cannabutter, softened (see p. 28)

¼ cup water (filtered is best), plus more if needed

1 tbsp freshly squeezed lemon juice

1 flattened tsp baking powder

1 tsp salt

1 egg yolk, whisked

Sesame seeds, for garnish

1|

Preheat the oven to 350°F. Line a baking sheet with parchment paper.

2|

In a wide mixing bowl, combine all ingredients except the egg yolk and sesame seeds. Using your hands, knead the dough thoroughly for a few minutes, making sure its texture is oily and comfortable to work with. (If need be, add a little more water or flour.)

3|

Divide the dough into 3 equal pieces and roll each to a thin, long cylinder. Cut each cylinder into 6 to 7 equal parts and connect the ends of each, creating a tiny bagel shape.

4|

Place the tiny bagels on the prepared baking sheet and brush with the egg yolk. Generously sprinkle sesame seeds over each niblet.

5|

Bake for 30 to 35 minutes, or until the edges brown. Remove from the oven and wait for the Abadi niblets to cool completely.

6|

Enjoy. Store in an airtight container for up to 2 weeks.

Potency: *If you're using a 15% THC strain, this recipe yields approximately 20 mg of THC per serving. See how to calculate potency on p. 24.*

Moderate   70min   Vegan

HEALTHY CANNACKERS
(CANNABIS CRACKERS)

These crackers are easy to make, cheap, healthy, and have a long shelf life—you really can't ask for much more. I make these when I'm going on one of my backpacking trips, as they can keep for days without refrigeration. They're great with one of the dip recipes (see chapter 5), or with an evening tea and funny conversations.

 25 Crackers

1 cup all-purpose flour

1 cup whole wheat flour

⅓ cup flax seeds

⅓ cup oatmeal

½ cup sesame seeds

½ cup raw sunflower seeds, peeled

2 tsp baking powder

1 tbsp salt

⅓ cup canna-oil (based on canola oil, see p. 30)

¾ cup cold water

1|

In the bowl of a stand mixer fitted with the paddle attachment, combine all ingredients except the canna-oil and water and mix slowly for 1 minute.

2|

While continuing to mix, gradually add the canna-oil and water to the bowl and mix for 1 minute more, or until the mixture reaches an even, dough-like consistency. Cover tightly with plastic wrap and refrigerate for 30 minutes.

3|

Preheat the oven to 350°F. Line a baking sheet with parchment paper.

4|

Turn out the dough onto a sheet of parchment paper. Working from the center outward, roll the dough into a 1/8-inch-thick (or thinner) rectangle. If the dough starts to shrink back as you roll it, set aside to rest, uncovered, for 5 minutes, and then continue.

5|

Using a pizza cutter or a sharp knife, cut the dough into cracker-sized (roughly 1 inch by 1½ inches) rectangles.

6|

Transfer the crackers to the prepared baking sheet; it's fine to crowd the crackers very close to each other. Bake for 30 minutes, or until the crackers are crisp and lightly browned. Remove from the oven and set aside to cool completely. Serve.

Potency: If you're using a 15% THC strain, this recipe yields approximately 15 mg of THC per serving. See how to calculate potency on p. 24.

Simple   20min   Vegan

CANNASCHUG
(SPICY CILANTRO CHUTNEY)

*I used to live next to a street market, and every day, I'd savor its scents of
garlic and cilantro. At some point, I reached an agreement with a local vendor:
I'd make him a generous portion of my Schug, and in exchange he'd be extra
generous with the pricing of my ingredients. When I got into canna-cooking, it
was obvious to me that this recipe was going to be an experiment. So here you
go: an easy and quick special twist on this Yemenite delight.*

2 bunches cilantro, washed thoroughly and dried
  (this is really important)

10 garlic cloves, peeled

2–3 jalapeño peppers, stemmed (be sure to use
  the seeds)

½ cup canola oil

3 tbsp cannabis-infused canola oil (see p. 30)

1 tbsp freshly squeezed lemon juice

½ tsp ground cumin

Salt and freshly ground black pepper, to taste

1|

In the bowl of a food processor fitted with the
"S" blade, combine the cilantro, garlic, and
jalapeño peppers and process until the mixture
is even.

2|

While processing, gradually drizzle in the canola oil
and the cannabis-infused canola oil. The mixture will
slowly reach a pesto-like consistency. Last, add the
lemon juice and cumin and season with the salt and
black pepper. Taste and adjust the seasoning
as needed.

3|

Use immediately or keep refrigerated in a sealed
container for up to 2 weeks.

*Potency: If you're using a 15% THC strain, this entire
recipe yields approximately 225 mg of THC. See how to
calculate potency on p. 24.*

Simple   50min   Vegan

INFUSED CHIMICHURRI SAUCE

I can think of no better marinade and sauce for meat than chimichurri. This gift from South American cuisine is perfect with a smidge of cannabis-infused oil. The parsley, garlic, and vinegar tastes are so dominant, you'll have no way of knowing that this is quite a potent recipe. I created this version when I was asked to serve intoxicating and savory aperitifs; just cut a good ½-inch ribeye into cubes and immerse it in this amazing, delicious sauce. It's double the fun, guaranteed!

1 bunch Italian parsley, finely chopped

½ onion, peeled and finely chopped

½ red bell pepper, finely chopped

10 garlic cloves, peeled and finely chopped

10 mint leaves, finely chopped

1 small red jalapeño pepper, finely chopped (include the seeds if you're into spicy stuff)

½ tsp dried oregano

1 tsp salt

½ cup canola oil, plus more as needed

1 cup warm water, plus more as needed

¾ cup white vinegar, plus more as needed

4 tbsp cannabis-infused canola oil (see p. 30)

2 tsp honey

1|

In a mixing bowl, combine the parsley, onion, bell pepper, garlic, mint, jalapeño pepper, oregano, and salt and mix well.

2|

Now for the liquids and honey: combine them in a mixing bowl and stir them together somewhat aggressively—you want all the ingredients to blend into one another. If you feel the chimichurri is too thick, you can add more liquid; just maintain the oil/water/vinegar ratio.

3|

Combine the contents of both mixing bowls and refrigerate the chimichurri for at least 30 minutes before serving. Mix each time before serving.

Potency: If you're using a 15% THC strain, this entire recipe yields approximately 300 mg of THC. See how to calculate potency on p. 24.

Simple   40min   Vegetarian

CANNA-PESTO MOZZARELLA SWIRLS

This great savory dish has a sweet kick to it! It's one of those easy recipes that definitely offers a great return for quick and effortless cooking. Oh… and as long as you're making a mess in the kitchen, I'd advise doubling the pesto ingredients, so you have some extra for later use. It should keep for up to 1 month if you store it in a sterilized, sealed container.

 8

1 cup fresh basil leaves

¼ cup high-quality parmesan cheese

2 garlic cloves

2 hearty tbsp roasted pine nuts

Salt, to taste (optional)

¼ cup cannabis-infused olive oil (see recipe on p. 30)

1 (10-inch x 15-inch) sheet frozen shortcrust

1 cup shredded mozzarella cheese

1|

Preheat the oven to 375°F. Line a baking sheet with parchment paper.

2|

Start with the pesto: In the bowl of a food processor fitted with the "S" blade, combine the basil, parmesan cheese, garlic, pine nuts, and salt, if using, and process on high for 1 minute, or until a coarse mixture forms. Reduce the speed to low and slowly add the cannabis-infused olive oil in a steady stream. Taste and adjust the seasoning as needed.

3|

Place the thawed pastry sheet on a clean work surface. Spread the pesto in a thin layer over the sheet of pastry and top with the shredded mozzarella cheese.

4|

Roll the pastry into a tight log. Chill the log, seam side down, for 15 minutes in the freezer.

5|

Immediately slice the log into eight 1-inch rounds using a sharp, wet knife. If the dough is too soft, return it to the freezer for a few minutes.

6|

Place the swirls on the prepared baking tray and bake for 20 minutes, or until they turn golden and puffed. Remove from the oven and chill before serving.

Potency: If you're using a 15% THC strain, this recipe yields approximately 37 mg of THC per serving. See how to calculate potency on p. 24.

Moderate   *70min*   *Vegetarian*

CROSTINI WITH CHARRED EGGPLANT & ROASTED CANNA-GARLIC SPREAD

This is a great starter dish to fuel a night of euphoric conversations. The garlic spread is a perfect carrier for the THC due to its distinct flavor, which acts as a great disguise for the cannabis aftertaste. If you're into a cheekier culinary zing, replace the tomato with pomegranate seeds.

8

Extra-virgin olive oil, as needed

1 large eggplant, cut lengthwise in half

2 whole large garlic heads (do not break into cloves)

8 (¾-inch-thick) slices fresh baguette

2 tbsp cannabis-infused olive oil (see p. 30)

2 tbsp freshly squeezed lemon juice

1 tsp dried oregano

Salt and freshly ground black pepper, to taste

4 oz good-quality crumbled feta cheese

1 medium tomato, finely chopped

1 cup arugula leaves

1|

Preheat the oven to 350°F. Line a baking sheet with parchment paper and grease it with a thin layer of the olive oil.

2|

Place the eggplant halves face down on the prepared baking sheet. Poke a few holes in the halves using a fork and roast for 55 minutes. Remove from the oven and set aside.

3|

Halve the garlic heads across the middle. Drizzle them with the olive oil and place them on four individual sheets of aluminum foil. Bring all four corners of each foil together and pinch gently, making sure the garlic is sealed inside. Roast for 45 minutes (the garlic will be soft and slightly brown in color when it's done). Remove from the oven and set aside.

4|

Spread a generous amount of the olive oil on each of the bread slices and place them on a rack. Bake for 10 minutes, or until they turn a beautiful golden color. Remove from the oven.

5|

Squeeze the roasted garlic cloves out into a small mixing bowl (they should fall out easily). While the garlic is still hot, add the cannabis-infused olive oil, lemon juice, and oregano and mash them all together to a paste. Season with the salt and black pepper; taste and adjust the seasoning as desired.

6|

Using a spoon, scrape the eggplant meat into a small bowl.

7|

To build the crostini, spread the roasted garlic paste on one side of each slice of toast. Add a generous amount of the eggplant meat to each slice and sprinkle the feta cheese and tomato bits over each. Last, add arugula leaves to each and serve immediately.

Potency: If you're using a 15% THC strain, this recipe yields approximately 18 mg of THC per serving. See how to calculate potency on p. 24.

Simple   90min   Vegetarian

HALLOUMI CHEESE, WEED AND FRUIT SKEWERS

This recipe got into the book due to popular demand. There hasn't been a single time that I've made it for friends and not been showered with rave reviews. It's highly recommended for sunny and fun outdoor social events.

8-10

1 cup brandy

½ cup pineapple juice

5 tbsp cannabis-infused honey (see p. 39)

Assorted fruit cubed or sliced for skewering
 (strawberries, fresh pineapple, pear, apple, peach,
 banana, kiwi, or persimmon)

6 oz halloumi cheese, cut into ½-inch cubes

3 tbsp light brown sugar, densely packed (optional)

¼ tsp ground cinnamon

¼ tsp ground allspice

¼ tsp freshly grated nutmeg

12 small bamboo skewers

1|

In a medium bowl, whisk together the brandy,
pineapple juice, and 4 tbsp of the cannabis-infused
honey until the mixture reaches an even,
liquid consistency.

2|

Place the fruit and halloumi cheese cubes in the
brandy mixture and refrigerate, stirring occasionally
to make sure all are equally saturated, for 60 to 90
minutes. If using bamboo skewers, it's best to soak
them in water at the same time to prevent them
from burning on the grill.

3|

Preheat a grill to roughly 350°F.

4|

In a small bowl, combine the brown sugar (if using),
cinnamon, allspice, and nutmeg.

5|

Alternate pieces of the fruit and halloumi cheese
on the skewers. Dust them generously with the
spice mixture.

6|

Once all the skewers are ready, place them on
the preheated open grill and grill for 5 minutes
on each side, until the cheese and fruit get a nice
caramelized tan. Brush the skewers with the brandy
marinade and the remaining cannabis-infused
honey while on the grill (don't throw away what's
left of the marinade – you can definitely find a
creative way of using it on a later occasion). Remove
from the grill.

7|

Serve and enjoy.

*Potency: It's impossible to calculate the potency
of this recipe for each serving. The entire marinade
contains roughly 250 mg of THC (if you use a 15%
THC strain), so assume that each skewer can give
you a nice, light buzz, but nothing more. See how to
calculate potency on p.24.*

Simple *10min* *Vegetarian*

WEED CHAI MASALA LATTE

This is a comforting fusion of Indian and Western culinary tastes. The strong flavor of freshly roasted spices serves as great camouflage for the cannabis aftertaste. If you don't have the spices on hand or just want to shortcut around some time and effort, use three Chai Masala tea bags in place of the first five ingredients, but I find this significantly reduces the flavor experience.

 4

1 cinnamon stick

4 cardamom pods

2 cloves

3 peppercorns

2 black tea teabags (Ceylon tea is best, but English Breakfast works as well)

1 (¼-inch) piece ginger, peeled

2 cups water

2 cups whole milk

2 tsp cannabutter (see p. 28), plus more if you desire more potency

2 tbsp Grade A maple syrup or brown sugar (optional)

Pinch ground cinnamon, for dusting

1|

In a dry, heavy skillet over medium heat, toast the cinnamon stick, cardamom, cloves, and peppercorns for a few minutes, or until a strong fragrance rises from the skillet. Remove from the heat and set aside to rest for a few minutes.

2|

In a small pot over medium-high heat, bring the water to a boil. Reduce the heat to very low, add the toasted spices and ginger, and let it simmer for a good 10 minutes.

3|

Meanwhile, in a second small pot over low heat, combine the milk, cannabutter, and maple syrup and cook, stirring constantly, until the sugar and butter have completely dissolved and the milk is lightly steaming. Remove from the heat and whisk or use an electric frother to foam the milk.

4|

Strain the tea among 4 teacups and then add the milk to each, making sure to leave a bit of froth to top each of the teacups. Dust each serving with the cinnamon and voila! Enjoy!

Potency: If you're using a 15% THC strain, this recipe yields approximately 17 mg of THC per serving. See how to calculate potency on p. 24.

Simple 10min Vegetarian

HERBAL TEA
(LITERALLY)

This classic herbal tea infusion is infused with… an additional herb.

 1

1 large cup water

1 tsp cannabis-infused honey (see recipe on page 39)

Honey, to taste (optional)

Generous assortment of fresh herbs* for tea, such as mint, lemon verbena, sage, lemon balm, etc.

1 lemon slice, for garnish

1|

Add the water to a small pot and bring to a boil.

2|

Add the cannabis-infused honey and regular honey, if using to sweeten the deal a bit.

3|

Reduce the heat to low, add the herbs, and let simmer for 2-3 minutes, stirring frequently until the honey dissolves completely. Remove from the heat.

4|

Let the tea rest for an additional 2-3 minutes.

5|

Strain the tea (or not) and garnish with the lemon slice. Drink up!

* You can also use dried herb leaves inside a loose tea container or tea bag.

Potency: If you're using a 15% THC strain, this recipe yields approximately 16 mg of THC per serving. See how to calculate potency on p. 24.

So simple, so healthy, and so tasty—what else does one need from a recipe? I find that this is a great introductory recipe for edible beginners. It's extremely easy to control the dosage, both by limiting the ingredients and by not finishing the drink, and it's great fun for both the mind and the taste buds.

Preparing these smoothies is really the easiest thing possible- place all the ingredients in a blender and blend till you reach that even, liquidy texture, and drink up.

THE CLASSIC:
BANANA-STRAWBERRY DELIGHT

 2

12–20 fresh or frozen strawberries, stemmed

2 bananas, peeled

1 cup ice cubes

1 cup plain yogurt or soy yogurt

1 cup water or dairy, almond, soy, or coconut milk

1 tbsp marijuana-infused honey (see p. 39)

1 tsp chia seeds to add after the blend (optional but recommended)

Potency: If you're using a 15% THC strain, this recipe yields approximately 25 mg of THC per serving. See how to calculate potency on p. 24.

THE REHYDRATOR:
WATERMELON, MINT & COCONUT

 2

3 cups watermelon chunks

2 cups pure coconut water, with no additives

1 cup frozen strawberries

1 cup ice cubes

10 fresh mint leaves

1 tbsp cannabis-infused coconut oil (see p. 33)

2 tsp freshly squeezed lime juice

1 tsp chia seeds (add after the blend)

Potency: If you're using a 15% THC strain, this recipe yields approximately 26 mg of THC per serving. See how to calculate potency on p. 24.

THE DETOXIFIER:
POMEGRANATE, BERRIES & SPINACH

 2

1½ cups coconut milk

1½ cups pomegranate seeds

1 cup frozen berry mix

1 cup fresh spinach leaves

1 cup ice cubes

1 banana

1 tbsp cannabis-infused coconut oil
  (see recipe on p. 33)

1 tbsp flax seeds

1 tsp honey

Potency: If you're using a 15% THC strain, this recipe yields approximately 26 mg of THC per serving. See how to calculate potency on p. 24.

THE EXOTIC:
MANGO LASSI

 2

2 cups ripe fresh mango, frozen mango, or mango pulp

2 cups plain yogurt

1 cup whole milk

1 cup ice cubes

1 tbsp marijuana-infused honey (see p. 39)

2 tbsp honey

Dash ground cardamom (optional)

Potency: If you're using a 15% THC strain, this recipe yields approximately 25 mg of THC per serving. See how to calculate potency on p. 24.

COOKING FOR THE MUNCHIES

Given the fact that marijuana consumption's legitimacy has increased dramatically in recent years—both legally and culturally speaking, society must prepare for what will surely follow: a munchies epidemic. When we hit that inevitable munchies stage, even the most disciplined among us may reach for a bag of chips or some candy bars. That's not to say that ready-to-eat, packaged comfort food is necessarily bad (it is, but I'm being politically correct here), but more often than not, we find ourselves regretting a gluttonous binge after the fact.

But fear not: help is here. The next chapters cater to those who want their munchies' experience to enhance their weed experience—not the opposite. Whether you're feeling adventurous, hosting others, wanting be super healthy, or treating yourself to some comfort food, you'll find a bunch of ideas here that will uplift your taste buds along with your spirit. Oh, and for those of you who are already high up there that have suddenly decided it's a good time to start cooking—there's a few super-tasty and creative ideas for you, too!

In short: your search is over. It's time to get cooking.

THE MUNCHIES

DEFINING THE MUNCHIES

One of the most common side effects of consuming marijuana, other than a sensation of euphoria, is a surge in appetite. This surge is what we in the industry call "the munchies."

While the munchies are great news for medicinal users who have trouble eating due to various health reasons, recreational users may find this phenomenon challenging for the waistline. At the time of the publication of this book, *Urban Dictionary* defined the munchies as "when you get hungry after smoking weed. Usually people will eat a lot of junk food." That's exactly what this book aims to abolish.

The cannabis industry has tried, unsuccessfully so far, to genetically modify strains that lessen this effect. But I say, let's not risk any interference in this gift of experience. Instead, just learn to control yourself. Don't get me wrong: I am completely aware that this poses a serious challenge to some of us (myself included). But if controlled, the munchies can actually work in your favor, as they enhance both your taste buds and your adventurous spirit (see Chapter 4: Unorthodox Combinations).

WHY IS THIS HAPPENING?

Marijuana's active ingredient, tetrahydrocannabinol (try saying that three times fast), which is kindly abbreviated as THC, both rewards you with a great euphoric sensation and increases your hunger. Your body naturally creates cannabinoids, which affect, in part, your levels of hunger. THC stimulates your brain, triggering the release of hormones that make you feel hungry even when you're far from it. There are a few explanations as to why this happens.

Some studies show that THC may significantly increase your ability to smell food and enjoy its taste, which can explain not only your hunger but also your increased sense of adventure. Also, being the animals that we are, most people tend to favor high-fat, high-carb foods when they encounter a feeling of starvation (even a fake one), so this is an almost natural reaction.

Typically, when your hunger is satisfied, your brain will signal your mouth to stop munching. Marijuana interferes with that natural process. Scientists now believe that cannabis initiates a chemical process that reverses the process and instead makes the brain continuously signal hunger.

SIX RULES FOR DEALING WITH THE MUNCHIES

RULE #1:
PLAN AHEAD

Face it: You are going to eat. If the munchies have a strong grip on you and you find yourself regretful afterward, plan ahead about what you're going to eat and have it readily available.

RULE #2:
BE SUPPORTED

If you're smoking with company, get support. Let your compadres know what you'd like to eat and, more importantly, when you should stop eating. Don't be ashamed. We're all in this together, and we're all human. I find that just telling people what my boundaries are keeps me in line without requiring any interference.

RULE #3:
EAT HEALTHY

You can do worse than chugging a bowl of kale and baby carrots. Have healthy alternatives ready. Put a bowl of fruit nearby and have a pitcher of water and a thermos of hot tea readily available.

RULE #4:
EAT MINDFULLY

Get your hippie on! When you're high up there, you can choose to enjoy your food more. Yes, it's up to you! If you find yourself with a dish that is worthy of appreciation, slow down. Take a bite and let the taste linger. Being high contributes to this mindful eating. Chew meditatively. If you do, you'll be rewarded with a better appreciation of the food, and you'll feel more satisfied as you chew slower.

RULE #5:
TIME YOUR MEAL

Be strategic. If you consume cannabis before you normally eat a meal, you let the munchies mingle with your normal appetite and make it easier to control the negative impact. Just don't get too complacent, and follow rule number one religiously.

RULE #6:
IF ALL ELSE FAILS, CONSIDER GOING TO BED

If you find yourself about to surrender to the hunger and stuff yourself to an undesirable extent, just go to bed. Take an apple or a slice of pizza with you and get cozy under a blanket. Luckily, smoking also makes you lazy, so chances are, you're not getting up from that position any time soon.

Whether it's due to the augmented sensory input or the depressed threshold for taste that comes with taking a few puffs, some foods just taste better after one has embellished oneself. In fact, some are either so much better or so much different (and better) when consumed under the influence that it's a culinary sin to not give them a try. For like-minded gastronomic explorers, this chapter offers an adventurous journey into the intricate combination of weird recipes I've tested and tasted while smoking a joint.

Cannabis elevates not only your levels of happiness, but also your taste buds. Combine that with the fact that it'll make you more open-minded to experiment with unorthodox food, and these recipes will be perfect for you.

Some of the recipes that follow are quite common in various cuisines from around the world, and some are a result of yours truly's dedicated trial-and-error activities. But if you want to do it right—and follow my advice here—don't just eat the food. Rather, take a "weird combination" bite, close your eyes, and fully absorb the contradiction. You might just fall in love…

04.
Unorthodox
Combinations

Advanced   50min   Meaty

RIBEYE NIBLETS WITH RED ONION MARMALADE

I don't think there's much to say here beyond the fact that this is one of our all-time favorite munchies. The steak, the garlic-infused butter, the phenomenal tangy-sweet red onion jam—just give us a joint, and there's nothing more we really need in life. I recommend making more of the onion marmalade, as it goes perfectly with many dishes... just saying...

 4

For the onion marmalade:

2 large red onions, peeled and thinly sliced into
   half circles
¼ cup canola oil
½ cup packed light brown sugar
½ cup dry red wine
3 tbsp balsamic vinegar

1|

Make the onion marmalade: In a large skillet over medium heat, warm the canola oil. Add the onions and sauté until they become transparent.

2|

Reduce the heat to low and add the remaining marmalade ingredients. Cook, stirring every few minutes, for 40 to 50 minutes, or until all the liquid has evaporated and the mixture has a creamy, sweet texture. Remove from the heat and set aside to cool to room temperature; store in the refrigerator.

3|

Make the niblets: Remove the steak from the refrigerator for at least 10 to 15 minutes before the cooking time and season it generously with the salt and black pepper.

For the niblets:

1 (1-lb, 1-inch-thick) ribeye steak
Sea salt and freshly ground black pepper, to taste
4 tbsp olive oil
1 head garlic, halved
3 tbsp unsalted butter
1 small bunch fresh thyme

4|

In a large, heavy skillet over medium heat, warm the olive oil. Gently add the steak to the skillet (watch out, as the oil will be hot). Cook for 2 minutes on each side.

5|

Add the butter, garlic, and thyme to the skillet. Once the butter melts, give the skillet a few good shakes to spread the love equally.

6|

Continue cooking the steak, turning it over every 2 to 3 minutes, for another 8 minutes for medium doneness. Remove from the heat.

7|

Slice the steak into 1-inch cubes and serve with a generous amount of onion marmalade on each niblet.

Moderate   45min   Vegetarian

CRISPY GOAT CHEESE WITH BEET JAM AND A SURPRISE

I must admit that I'm super proud of this dish, which is one of my most notoriously crazed inventions. The creamy texture of the goat cheese, along with the panko crunch, the spicy throwaway, and, finally, the bittersweet beet jam, all add up to a very appetizing party.

12

For the beet jam:

1 cup confectioners' sugar

¼ cup warm water

Freshly squeezed juice and freshly grated zest of
  ½ lemon

3 medium red beets, peeled and cut into very
  small cubes

1 ripe pear, peeled and cut into very small cubes (an
  apple will also work)

1 stick cinnamon

1|

Make the beet jam: In a small pot over high heat,
combine the sugar, water, and lemon juice and zest
and bring to a boil.

2|

Reduce the heat to medium and add the beets, pear,
and cinnamon stick. Cook, stirring occasionally, for
35 minutes, or until it reaches a jam-like consistency.
Remove from the heat.

3|

Set aside to cool for a couple of hours before serving
(it will keep it in the fridge for up to 2 weeks).

4|

Make the goat cheese: In a skillet over high heat,
warm the canola oil. Add the jalapeño halves and fry
for 2 to 3 minutes on each side, or just before they
change color. Remove the jalapeño halves from the
pan but keep the skillet over the heat.

5|

Divide each jalapeño half in half again and place
them on a plate lined with paper towels to drain.

For the goat cheese:

1 cup canola oil

3 large jalapeño peppers, halved lengthwise, stemmed,
  and seeded

1 (9-ounce) log fresh goat cheese

½ cup all-purpose flour

1 whole large egg, beaten

1 cup breadcrumbs

6|

Using thread, cut the goat cheese log into 12 equal
slices (you can use a knife, but thread is much neater
and easier).

7|

Place the flour, beaten egg, and breadcrumbs in 3
separate wide, shallow bowls. Dip each piece of goat
cheese first in the flour, then in the beaten egg, and
then in the breadcrumbs, making sure you shake off any
excess after each dip.

8|

As you finish breading each slice, place each cheese
slice in the hot oil. Fry for 3 minutes, just until the
breadcrumbs become a brownish-golden color. Remove
the fried slices to a paper-towel lined plate to drain. Once
all of the slices have been fried, remove from the heat.

9|

Arrange the fried goat cheese slices on a platter. Place
a piece of fried jalapeño on top of each piece and top
each with a teaspoon of the beet jam. Serve and step
aside, as there will be a galloping stampede for this
dangerously tasty dish.

Moderate   *25min*   *Meaty*

CARAMELIZED PINEAPPLE & GRILLED CHICKEN QUESADILLAS WITH SPICY STRAWBERRY DIP

This recipe provides nothing short of a flavor symphony. Just take a bite, close your eyes, and let it take you on a delicious journey that will both challenge and excite your taste buds.

 2

For the strawberry dip:

10 strawberries, stemmed

1 jalapeño pepper, stemmed but seeds retained

½ cup fresh cilantro leaves and stems

¼ small red onion

1 tbsp freshly squeezed lime juice

Salt and freshly ground black pepper, to taste

For the quesadillas:

1 tbsp unsalted butter

¼ small pineapple, peeled and cubed

2 tbsp light brown sugar

1 tbsp freshly squeezed lemon juice

1 tbsp olive oil

½ tsp chipotle chili powder

½ tsp smoked paprika

1 (6-8-ounce) boneless, skinless chicken breast

2 flour tortillas

1 small poblano pepper, seeded, diced, and
   thinly sliced

1 (6-ounce) piece Monterey jack cheese, freshly grated

½ cup coarsely chopped fresh cilantro

1|

Make the strawberry dip: Combine all the ingredients in the jug of a blender and blend until the texture is even and smooth (if you like a smoother texture, run it through a food mill or chinois). Taste and adjust the seasoning if desired.

2|

Make the quesadillas:
In a skillet over low heat, warm the butter. Add the pineapple cubes, brown sugar, and lemon juice and cook, stirring constantly, for 7 minutes. The pineapple cubes will slowly brown as they absorb the buttery caramel (you can taste one, but leave the rest for the real deal). Remove from the heat and set aside to cool slightly.

3|

Preheat a grill to medium-high heat.

4|

In a small mixing bowl, combine the olive oil, chipotle chili powder, and paprika. Dip the chicken breast in the mixture until it is evenly coated.

5|

Place the chicken on the grill and cook for 4 to 5 minutes on each side (slice it a bit to check that it's cooked through). Remove from the grill and slice into ¼-inch slices.

6|

Reduce the grill heat to low. Place 1 tortilla on a plate and arrange the caramelized pineapple slices on top. Add the chicken slices and poblano pepper and top with the cheese and cilantro. When you're done, gently place the second tortilla on top.

7|

Slowly slide the quesadilla off the plate and onto the grill. Grill, uncovered, for about 3 minutes. Using a plate or a large spatula, flip the quesadilla over and grill for another 2 to 3 minutes on the other side. Remove from the grill, slice up "pizza style," and serve.

Simple · 20min · Vegetarian

FRIED PICKLES WITH SPICY HORSERADISH DIP

Yup, we're deep-frying pickles! I know that some of you Southerners might find this recipe unchallenging in terms of its culinary creativity, but for the rest of us, this just seems weird. However, this combo of pickled dill and horseradish offers what I call a "food knockout." It always goes like this: "Are these pickles??!!" After a bite, it always ends with "I can't believe these are pickles! They're so good...."

 5

For the spicy horseradish dip:

½ cup high-quality mayonnaise

3 generous tbsp finely grated horseradish

2 tbsp finely chopped fresh chives

1 clove garlic, minced

1 tsp sweet paprika

1 tsp whole-grain mustard

For the pickles:

1 cup all-purpose flour

2 tsp Cajun seasoning

½ tsp cayenne pepper

1 whole large egg, beaten

1 cup breadcrumbs

Canola oil, for deep frying

2 cups sliced dill pickles, drained and patted dry

Salt and freshly ground black pepper, to taste

1|

Make the spicy horseradish dip: Mix together all the ingredients in a small mixing bowl. Taste and adjust as desired and set aside.

2|

Make the pickles: In a wide, shallow bowl, mix together the flour, Cajun seasoning, salt, black pepper, and cayenne pepper. Place the beaten egg and breadcrumbs in 2 separate, wide, shallow bowls.

3|

In a skillet over medium heat, warm the canola oil (when a drop of water hits it, it should sizzle loudly but not make popping sounds).

4|

Dip each pickle slice first in the flour mixture, then in the beaten egg, and then in the breadcrumbs, making sure you shake off any excess after each dip. Drop the coated pickle slices into the hot oil and fry for 3 to 4 minutes, or until they take on a golden-brownish color. Remove from the heat and transfer the pickles to a plate lined with paper towels to drain. Serve hot with the spicy horseradish dip.

Simple   15min   Vegetarian

STRAWBERRY, TOMATO & MINT SALAD

This great, weird little recipe is perfect for a hot day. I find that we don't experiment often enough with combining sweet and savory flavors. This salad offers it all: crunchy, sweet, savory, tangy, soft, hard, and even a touch of bitterness. When combined, they offer a delicious, somewhat metaphysical expedition that's definitely worth the effort.

 4

For the vinaigrette:

3 tbsp extra-virgin olive oil

1 tbsp good (preferably aged)

balsamic vinegar

1 clove garlic, crushed

1 tsp honey

1 tsp freshly squeezed lemon juice

Sea salt and freshly ground black pepper, to taste

For the salad:

12 oz cherry tomatoes, halved

12 oz strawberries, stemmed and halved

1 (8 oz) piece fresh soft goat cheese, crumbled
  or sliced

1 small bunch fresh arugula leaves

1 small bunch fresh mint leaves, stems discarded

Handful shelled pistachio nuts

1|

Make the vinaigrette: In a small mixing bowl, whisk together all the vinaigrette ingredients until the mixture is smooth.

2|

Make the salad: In a serving bowl, combine all of the ingredients. Add the vinaigrette and toss until the salad is well coated. Close your eyes and take a bite. You're welcome!

Moderate   25min   Meaty

SIRLOIN BITES IN A SPICED POMEGRANATE SAUCE

This is a great way to test your boundaries: the pomegranate sauce offers a rare fusion of sweet, spicy, and tangy flavors, and it goes great with an exploratory attitude. A neighbor of mine who had a pomegranate tree and a few extra pounds of fruit to spare inspired my research into the realm of pomegranate sauce. Since then, I've perfected my recipe with a lot of trial, taste, and error.

 4

1 cup pomegranate juice

¼ cup red wine

Freshly squeezed juice of 1 lemon

¼ cup raw sugar

2 cloves garlic, crushed

2 tbsp butter

1 tbsp chili flakes

1 tsp ground ginger

½ tsp ground coriander

2 tsp cornstarch

¼ cup warm water

1½ lb thick-cut sirloin steak

Sea salt and freshly ground black pepper, to taste

Canola oil, for frying

Fresh mint leaves, for garnish

1|

In a skillet over low heat, combine the tangy-sweet pomegranate juice and red wine and cook for 2 to 3 minutes. Add the lemon juice, sugar, garlic, butter, chili flakes, ginger, and coriander, and cook, stirring constantly, until the ingredients dissolve together into a sauce. Continue to cook for 10 minutes, or until the sauce thickens a bit.

2|

In a measuring cup, whisk together the water and cornstarch and warm water until the cornstarch dissolves completely. Pour the mixture into the pan and cook for an additional 5 to 7 minutes, or until the pomegranate sauce has thickened. Remove from the heat and set aside to cool.

3|

Generously season the steaks with the sea salt and black pepper.

4|

In a frying pan over medium heat, warm the canola oil. Add the steaks and cook for 5 minutes on each side. Remove from the heat.

5|

Slice the steak into ½-inch cubes and return them to the pan. Add the pomegranate sauce and return the pan to low heat. Cook for 5 minutes. Remove from the heat; serve and enjoy garnished with the mint leaves.

Simple   35min   Vegan

GRAPE SALSA

Undoubtedly, this is one of the great hidden gems in the realm of salsas. For the life of me, I don't get why people discriminate against grapes when it comes to savory dishes. I can't think of a single time that I've pulled out this baby alongside a bag of chips and didn't get enthusiastic reviews. So sure, the reviewers were, for the most part, at various stages of being high when they tried it, but you know how it goes—in goes the weed, out comes the truth….

 4

1 cup seedless green grapes, quartered

1 cup seedless red grapes, quartered

1 Persian cucumber, peeled and finely chopped

1 red onion, finely chopped

1 jalapeño pepper, stemmed, seeded, and
   finely chopped

Freshly squeezed juice of 1 lime

3 tbsp finely chopped fresh cilantro leaves and stems

2 cloves garlic, minced

1 tbsp red wine vinegar

1 tsp oregano (optional)

Pinch salt

Freshly ground black pepper, to taste

Combine all the ingredients in a mixing bowl and toss until very well combined. Store in the refrigerator for 1 hour before serving to allow the flavors to meld.

Grilled cheese sandwiches long ago ceased to be a standard dish in my house. Nowadays, I treat them more as a concept or a platform on which I can explore various creative cookeries. It's a perfect medium to go crazy with savory, sweet, bitter, and even spicy elements.

To make a proper grilled cheese sandwich, use this basic recipe to make the following variations.

1|

Warm a dry grill pan over medium heat.

2|

Spread 1 tsp of the butter on 1 side of each slice of bread. Place the cheese and any other fillings you may have on the unbuttered side of 1 of the slices of bread. Top with the other slice of bread, buttered side up.

3|

Place the sandwich on the grill pan and cook for 2 to 4 minutes on each side, until you reached your desired level of crustiness. Remove from the heat and serve hot.

CARAMELIZED PEAR AND MANCHEGO

*I know many people who've added caramelized pears to their grilled
cheese and then had to face the harsh reality that this concoction wouldn't
necessarily be a part of their grilled cheeses going forward.*

1 medium soft pear, cored and diced (1 pear makes 4
sandwiches)

1 generous tbsp packed light brown sugar

1 tbsp + 1 tsp unsalted butter

Pinch ground cloves

2 slices high-quality sourdough bread

1 slice Manchego cheese

Make the caramelized pear: In a skillet over medium
heat, combine the pear, the sugar, and 1 tbsp of the
butter and sauté until the butter has melted and the
sugar has completely dissolved. Add the cloves and
stir until well combined. Stir well until the pear cubes
are completely coated. Remove from the heat and set
aside for 5 minutes.

GOAT CHEESE, BASIL & FIG PRESERVES

*In my opinion, goat cheese and figs are a super group. It's very hard to screw
up a dish that combines both....*

1 tsp unsalted butter, softened

2 slices challah or French brioche

1 (2 oz) piece fresh soft goat cheese

1 tbsp fig preserves

1 tsp thinly sliced fresh basil leaves

HONEY TRUFFLE AND GRUYÈRE

*For the unfortunates out there who don't truly appreciate truffles, this recipe
might not be a good fit. The like-minded rest will find, as I do, that truffles and
getting high work exquisitely well together.*

1 tsp honey

1 tsp fresh black truffle shavings or 1 pinch truffle salt

1 tsp unsalted butter, softened

2 slices multigrain bread

1 large slice Gruyère cheese

Moderate   *10min*   *Vegan*

AVOCADO & DARK CHOCOLATE PUDDING

If ever you find yourself sharing a spiritual journey with vegan friends and desiring to indulge them with something weird and sweet—this great recipe would be a perfect choice.

 5

2 large ripe (but not blackened) avocados, peeled, pitted, and mashed

½ cup unsweetened cocoa powder

⅓ cup date honey

⅓ cup coconut milk

1 tsp vanilla extract

Pinch nutmeg

Pinch sea salt

Banana slices, cocoa nibs, or blueberries, for garnish (optional)

1|

Combine all the ingredients in the jug of a blender and blend until the texture is even and silky smooth.

2|

Transfer the pudding to a bowl and refrigerate for at least 30 minutes.

3|

Serve cold. This pudding isn't super sweet, so if you like things on the sweet side, serve garnished with the banana slices, cocoa nibs, or blueberries.

Simple *5min* *Vegetarian*

VANILLA ICE CREAM WITH SEA SALT AND OLIVE OIL

This is an experiment we once shared with Andrea, a dear friend of ours from Italy, and that we've repeated many times since. This Italian anecdote is a go-to weird combination for us when we're sweet-toothing.

 1

2 scoops high-quality vanilla ice cream

1 tbsp extra-virgin olive oil

2 tbsp shelled pistachio nuts, walnuts, or hazelnuts

Pinch sea salt

Place the vanilla ice cream in a serving dish. Drizzle the olive oil on top and sprinkle over the nuts and salt.

Now dig in!

Simple   5min   Vegan

WALNUTS AND DATES

A Mediterranean treat. Quality ingredients are key here: to truly enjoy this weird combination, find fresh walnuts and large, soft dates.

 10

20 large, soft Medjool dates

10 fresh walnut halves

Using a small knife, cut open the side of each date. Without harming the dates, remove and discard the pits. Once all the pits have been removed, replace each with a walnut half. Serve.

Simple   5min   Vegetarian

COLD WATERMELON & FETA CHEESE

This dish, which is nearly a staple "end of the meal" in Mediterranean cuisines, has been completely ignored pretty much everywhere else in the world. For this recipe, use good-quality, fresh feta cheese and fresh, cold watermelon.

 5

1 small watermelon, very cold and cubed

1 lb high-quality feta cheese, cubed

Fresh mint leaves, for garnish (optional)

Freshly ground black pepper, to taste

Toothpicks

This is an extremely complicated recipe, so brace yourself: spear a cube of watermelon on a toothpick and add a cube of the feta on top of that. For the true adventurists, I'd recommend adding a couple of fresh mint leaves between the feta and watermelon. Season lightly with the black pepper and enjoy.

Beer Vegetable Tempura with Wasabi Dipping Sauce
-148-

Fried Avocado Dippers with Ranch-Style Dip
-150-

Spicy Roasted Red Pepper and Feta Concoction with Zucchini and Sweet Potato Tots
-154-

Tzatziki and Portabella Fries
-158-

Rainbow Tahini Variations (4 recipes)
-161-

Guacamole with Various Twists
-165-

Roasted Jalapeño Dipping Sauce with Baked Chicken Fingers
-167-

Spicy Drumsticks with Even-Spicier Dipping Sauce
-169-

Sweet and Savory Apple Salsas (2 recipes)
-170-

For some of us, the hunger that comes about when we hit the munchies stage is a relentless, nagging feeling. For others, a good old cup of tea and a couple of cookies might do the job.

I find this chapter to be extremely relevant to folks at both ends of the spectrum. Having a few tasty dips and some creative dippers on hand will allows avid munchers to pace themselves and lets the quickly satiated have something to nibble on.

Preparing a few dips for any exploratory, cannabis-infused conversation is typically a very safe bet, as it guarantees a perfect munch match. Trust me when I say I've sacrificed many a merry encounter while exploring various dips and dippers, which has culminated in this, a winning recipe list for adding delectable flavor to your excursion. All that's left for you to do, really, is to take out a few bowls and gear up for the journey.

05.
Dips and Dippers

Advanced   *20min*   *Vegetarian*

BEER VEGETABLE TEMPURA WITH WASABI DIPPING SAUCE

This Japanese staple is endowed with some fish-and-chips ambience, only without the fish and the chips! The trick to making the perfect beer tempura is to get the batter as light as possible: use ice-cold beer, prepare it right before you're about to use it, and do not overmix it.

For the tempura:

1 small sweet potato, peeled and thinly sliced

¾ cup ice-cold light beer

¾ cup + ½ cup rice flour (if you don't have it,
  all-purpose flour works as well)

1 tsp salt

1 tsp cayenne powder

Vegetable oil, for deep frying

8 asparagus spears, trimmed

1 large zucchini, thinly sliced

1 large onion, cut into ½-inch rings

For the wasabi dipping sauce:

6 healthy tbsp excellent-quality mayonnaise

1 clove garlic, minced

1 tsp wasabi powder

1 tsp water

Salt and freshly ground black pepper, to taste

1|

Make the tempura: Place the sweet potatoes in a bowl and microwave on high for 5 minutes.

2|

In a mixing bowl, combine the beer, ¾ cup of the rice flour, the salt, and the cayenne powder. Mix well but carefully, making sure not to foam up the beer and overflow the bowl. Set aside at room temperature for a good 10 minutes.

3|

In a large, deep, and heavy-bottomed pan over medium heat, warm 2 to 3 inches of the oil to 350°F—no hotter and no cooler. To test the temperature of the oil, you can either use a candy thermometer or drop a little bit of the batter into the hot oil. It should first sink and then within a few seconds float right to the top with some sizzle. If it doesn't float and sizzle, increase the heat; if it doesn't sink, decrease the heat.

4|

Place the remaining ½ cup of rice flour on a separate plate.

5|

Using tongs, dip the sweet potato slices, asparagus spears, and zucchini and onion slices in the rice flour and shake off to remove any excess. Next, dip each in the batter. Pick up each and let any excess batter drip off (the beer batter is denser than regular tempura batter, and you don't want to over-coat the vegetables). Repeat until all of the vegetables are coated.

6|

Drop the vegetables in the hot oil and deep-fry for 4 minutes each. Check to see if the vegetables are darkening quickly; if so reduce the heat. Remove the vegetables from the oil and set aside on a plate lined with paper towels to drain.

7|

Make the wasabi dipping sauce: In a small bowl, whisk together all of the ingredients. Season with the salt and black pepper.

8|

Serve the hot tempura vegetables with the wasabi dipping sauce.

Moderate   20min   Vegetarian

FRIED AVOCADO DIPPERS WITH RANCH-STYLE DIP

The creamy-on-the-inside/crispy-on-the-outside dippers are perfect if you're in a sinful mood. The first few times I made these, I literally ate almost all the slices as soon as they came out of the pan (despite the protests of my burnt tongue), so now I typically plan on making a double portion. You might want to do the same!

8

For the ranch-style dip:

¾ cup sour cream

¾ cup mayonnaise

1 small bunch fresh flat-leaf parsley leaves,
  finely chopped

1 small bunch fresh chives, finely chopped

1 small bunch fresh dill, stemmed and finely chopped

2 cloves garlic, minced

Salt and freshly ground black pepper, to taste

1|

Make the ranch-style dip: In a mixing bowl, whisk together all of the ingredients. Season with the salt and black pepper and store in the refrigerator until ready to serve.

2|

Place 3 wide, shallow bowls on the counter. In the first bowl, combine the flour, paprika, and garlic powder and season with the salt. Place the beaten eggs in the second bowl. Finally, place the panko breadcrumbs in the last bowl.

3|

Cut each avocado half into 4 slices (for a total of 24 slices).

4|

In a large, deep, and heavy-bottomed pan over medium heat, warm 3 to 4 inches of the oil to 350°F. To test the temperature of the oil, you can either use a candy thermometer or drop a little bit of the batter into the hot oil. It should first sink and then within a few seconds float right to the top with some sizzle.

For the avocado dippers:

1 cup all-purpose flour

½ tsp sweet paprika

½ tsp garlic powder

Salt, to taste

2 whole large eggs, beaten

1 cup panko breadcrumbs

3 hard but ripe avocados, skinned, pitted, and halved

Vegetable oil, for deep frying

If it doesn't float and sizzle, increase the heat; if it doesn't sink, decrease the heat.

5|

Using your hands, dip a batch of 4 of the avocado slices in the spiced flour. Shake off any excess flour and dip the slices in the eggs. Again, shake off any excess egg and dip the slices in the panko bowl. Make sure each avocado slice is well covered with the panko. Repeat until all of the slices have been dipped in all three bowls.

6|

Drop the breaded avocado slices in the hot oil and fry for 3 to 4 minutes, or until each slice is floating in the oil and is browned. Remove from the oil and set aside to drain on a plate lined with paper towels.

7|

Serve the avocado dippers with the ranch-style dip.

Note: for a healthier version of this recipe, skip the deep frying and place the breaded avocados on a baking tray lined with parchment paper. Bake at 450°F for 20 minutes.

Moderate   *2h*   *Vegetarian*

SPICY ROASTED RED PEPPER & FETA CONCOCTION WITH ZUCCHINI & SWEET POTATO TOTS

When I was nine years old, my father shared a version of this dish with me. He encouraged me to "be a man" and take a bite, even though it's super spicy. While we can definitely argue about his parenting style, this opened up a whole new world of spicy and yummy foods to me. I'll acknowledge that this isn't one of those "put some stuff in a bowl and mix well" type of dip, but it definitely compensates by being awesome. If you're a spicy food fan, this is a must for you.

 6

For the red pepper dip:

4 large red peppers

3 tbsp canola oil

5 cloves garlic peeled and finely chopped

1 hearty tbsp crushed red chili flakes

1 tsp cayenne pepper

1 oz good feta cheese crumbled

Salt, to taste

1 tsp coriander seeds (optional; it adds a bit of tanginess)

For the veggie tots (15–20 pieces):

1 large zucchini, coarsely grated

1 large sweet potato, peeled and coarsely grated

3 tsp salt

½ cup freshly grated mozzarella

½ cup panko breadcrumbs

⅓ cup finely chopped flat-leaf parsley

2 cloves garlic, minced

2 whole large eggs

Freshly ground black pepper, to taste

1|

Make the red pepper dip: Preheat the oven to 350°F.

2|

Place the red peppers on a baking sheet and bake for 1 hour, turning halfway through the cooking time (it's fine if the skin blackens).

3|

Carefully remove the roasted peppers and place them in a bowl. Cover the bowl with plastic wrap and set aside for at least 30 minutes.

4|

Peel the skin off the red peppers and discard the stems and seeds (don't rinse the roasted peppers, as doing so will take away from the taste). Thinly slice the peeled roasted peppers.

5|

In a skillet over high heat, warm the oil. Add the garlic, red chili flakes, and cayenne pepper and cook for 1 min.

6|

Reduce the heat to low and immediately add the roasted peppers to the pan before the garlic darkens. Simmer, stirring constantly, for 5 minutes. Remove from the heat.

7|

On a small plate, spread out the cubed feta cheese. Pour the contents of the skillet evenly on top of it. Set aside for at least 20 minutes before continuing with the rest of the recipe; if you prefer, you can refrigerate it and eat it cold.

8|

Make the tots: Preheat the oven to 400°F. Line a baking sheet with parchment paper.

9|

In a bowl, mix together the zucchini, the sweet potato, and 2 tsp of the salt. Set aside for 20 minutes, or until the salt has drawn out some of the moisture.

10|

Transfer veggies into a kitchen towel and twist it to drain out as much of the moisture as you can.

11|

In a large bowl, combine the drained vegetables with all of the remaining ingredients and form the mixture into even-sized tots. Arrange the tots on the prepared baking sheet.

12|

Bake for 35 minutes, or until the tots are nicely browned, turning the tots halfway through the cooking time. Remove from the oven.

13|

Serve hot with the roasted red pepper dip.

Simple   20min   Vegetarian

TZATZIKI & PORTABELLA FRIES

When I just started cooking, many moons ago, tzatziki was one of my first go-to recipes. It's a very simple recipe that always comes out awesome and leaves everyone happy and asking for more. This gift from the culinary Greek gods is sure to satisfy the cravings of hungry truth-seekers.

For the tzatziki:

2 cups plain Greek (if you don't have Greek, then
   regular plain) yogurt

1 cup sour cream

1 cucumber, peeled and finely chopped

1 small bunch fresh chives, finely chopped

2 tbsp extra-virgin olive oil

1–2 cloves garlic, crushed (start with 1, taste, and add
   more if needed)

Salt and white pepper, to taste

3 tbsp pine nuts, for garnish (optional)

1 tsp sweet paprika, for garnish (optional)

For the portabella fries:

½ cup all-purpose flour

Salt and freshly ground black pepper, to taste

2 whole large eggs, beaten

2 cups panko breadcrumbs

1 cup finely chopped fresh flat-leaf parsley leaves

2 tbsp finely chopped fresh mint leaves

Vegetable oil, for frying

6 large portabella mushrooms, sliced into ¼-inch
   "fingers"

1|

Make the tzatziki: In a mixing bowl, mix together all of the ingredients until evenly mixed. Season with the salt and white pepper and garnish with the pine nuts and paprika, if using. Store in the refrigerator until ready to serve.

2|

Make the portabella fries: Place 3 wide, shallow bowls on the counter. In the first bowl, place the flour. Season with the salt and black pepper. Place the beaten eggs in the second bowl. In the last bowl, combine the panko breadcrumbs and parsley and mint leaves.

3|

In a large, deep, and heavy-bottomed pan over medium-high heat, warm 4 inches of the oil to 350°F. To test the temperature of the oil, you can either use a candy thermometer or drop a little bit of the batter into the hot oil. It should first sink and then within a few seconds float right to the top with some sizzle. If it doesn't float and sizzle, increase the heat; if it doesn't sink, decrease the heat.

4|

Using your hands, dip each portabella slice in the flour. Shake off any excess flour and dip the slices in the eggs. Again, shake off any excess egg and dip the slices in the panko bowl. Make sure each portabella slice is well covered with the panko. Repeat until all of the slices have been dipped in all three bowls.

5|

Drop the portabella slices in the hot oil and fry for 2 to 4 minutes, or until each slice is golden. Remove from the oil and set aside to drain on a plate lined with paper towels.

6|

Serve the portabella slices with the tzatziki.

Tahini is one of the oldest and most popular Mediterranean dishes. This awesome sesame butter twist is perfect as a dip as it's both delicious and nourishing. The only thing I'll ask from you is to find a good, solid, raw tahini and not settle for the cheap stuff as it will make all the difference.

Rainbow Tahini Variations

PLAIN OLE TAHINI

1 cup excellent-quality raw tahini

1 cup room-temperature water

Freshly squeezed juice of ½ lemon

1 clove garlic, crushed

Salt and white pepper, to taste

In a mixing bowl, whisk together all the ingredients. Season with the salt and white pepper. Taste and fine tune the tahini's flavor by adding more of any of the ingredients.

GREEN TAHINI

This one is my wife Daphne's favorite subrecipe... and rightfully so.

1 cup fresh flat-leaf parsley leaves

½ cup fresh cilantro

1 cup Plain Ole Tahini

Freshly squeezed lemon juice, to taste (optional)

Crushed garlic, to taste (optional)

Salt, to taste (optional)

In the bowl of a food processor fitted with the "S" blade, combine all the ingredients and chop on high until the mixture is smooth and even. Taste and fine tune the tahini's flavor by adding more of any of the ingredients, including the optional choices. The greens have a lot of water in them, which will dilute the tahini—so you may need to add a bit of lemon juice, garlic or salt.

RED TAHINI

This slightly sweeter version is just as healthy.

1 medium beet

1 cup Plain Ole Tahini

1|

Preheat the oven to 350°F.

2|

Cut the stem off the beet and wrap it in aluminum foil. Place it on a baking sheet and roast for 1 hour. Remove from the oven.

3|

In the bowl of a food processor fitted with the "S" blade, process the roasted beet and the tahini on high until the mixture is smooth and even.

BABA GANOUSH

Roasted eggplant and tahini are a match made in heaven and a true Mediterranean treat.

1 medium eggplant

1 cup Plain Ole Tahini

1 small bunch fresh flat-leaf parsley chopped

3 tbsp pine nuts

Dash sweet paprika, or to taste

1|

Preheat a grill to high heat.

2|

Place the eggplant on the hot grill and grill for 30 minutes, turning it over halfway through the cooking time. Remove from the grill and set aside until cool enough to touch.

3|

Remove and discard the eggplant's stem and skin. Take your time here, as bits of charred eggplant skin really harm the taste.

4|

In a mixing bowl, combine the eggplant and tahini. Using a fork and knife, cut the eggplant to create a semi-even texture and mix together well.

5|

Sprinkle the mixture with the parsley, pine nuts, and paprika for an authentic look. If you really want to do it right, roast the pine nuts first in a dry frying pan for 2 minutes—it makes an enormous difference!

Simple   *10min*   *Vegan*

GUACAMOLE WITH VARIOUS TWISTS

One cannot write a chapter about dips and not mention the one to rule them all—guacamole. I often wondered what I could do to turn a regular guacamole recipe into a phenomenal one. After dozens of attempts, I determined that it all comes down to the minute details: the freshness of your ingredients, how finely you chop them, and how many twists you're ready to add to provide a distinctive flavor to your signature guac.

 4

3 ripe (but not overripe) avocados, pitted and peeled

2 not-too-ripe tomatoes (preferably roasted), finely chopped

½ red onion, finely chopped

¼ cup finely chopped fresh cilantro

1 jalapeño pepper, stemmed, seeded, and finely chopped (optional)

Freshly squeezed juice of 1 lime, plus more to taste

1 clove garlic, minced, plus more to taste

Salt and freshly ground black pepper, to taste

For the twists:

(to the above recipe, add 1 or more of the below)

½ green apple, peeled and finely chopped

½ cup corn (preferably roasted)

½ cup finely chopped mango and/or pineapple

4 strips bacon, crumbled

¼ cup feta cheese crumbles

Arils (seeds) of ¼ pomegranate

1|

Place the avocados in a large bowl. Using a fork, mash them into a paste or leave them with a chunkier texture, if your heart desires.

2|

Add the tomatoes, onion, cilantro, and jalapeño and stir until well combined. Season with the lime juice, garlic, salt, and black pepper. Taste and adjust the seasoning as desired.

3|

Add 1 or more of the twists listed and stir until well combined.

4|

Serve and enjoy.

Simple 35min Meaty

ROASTED JALAPEÑO DIPPING SAUCE WITH BAKED CHICKEN FINGERS

The jalapeño era of my life began the first time I successfully grew a few jalapeño pepper plants. I was very proud of my green thumb—but I didn't know what to do with so many spicy peppers. What followed were a few months of burning fingers and exciting, spicy experimentations. If you love spicy food, this dip is perfect for you! Enjoy...

 6

For the jalapeño dipping sauce:

2 tbsp canola oil

5–8 medium jalapeño peppers, seeded and finely chopped (depending on level of desired spiciness)

1 cup chopped fresh cilantro

2 cloves garlic

1 cup sour cream

4 green onions, stemmed and chopped

Freshly squeezed juice of 1 lime

1 tbsp sweet paprika

1 tsp salt plus more to taste

For the chicken fingers:

2 cups panko breadcrumbs

1 cup all-purpose flour

Salt and freshly ground black pepper, to taste

2 whole large eggs, beaten

1 tbsp mayonnaise

2 lb chicken breast tenders

1|

Make the jalapeño dipping sauce: In a skillet over medium heat, warm the canola oil. Throw in the jalapeños, and sauté, stirring well, until the jalapeños are slightly darkened. Remove from the heat.

2|

Combine the cilantro and garlic in the bowl of a food processor fitted with the "S" blade. Process on high until the mixture is even.

3|

In a large bowl, stir together the contents of the food processor bowl with the sautéed jalapeños, sour cream, green onions, lime juice, paprika, and salt. Taste and reseason as desired.

4|

Make the baked chicken fingers: Preheat the oven to 350°F. Line a baking sheet with parchment paper.

5|

In a dry pan over low-medium heat, toast the panko breadcrumbs for 3 minutes, tossing constantly, until they are lightly browned (take care not to over-toast them).

6|

Place 3 wide, shallow bowls on the counter. In the first bowl, place the flour. Season with the salt and black pepper. Combine the beaten eggs and the mayonnaise in the second bowl. In the last bowl, place the toasted panko breadcrumbs.

7|

Using your hands, dip each chicken tender in the flour. Shake off any excess flour and dip the slices in the eggs and mayonnaise. Again, shake off any excess egg/mayo mixture and dip the slices in the panko bowl. Make sure each piece of chicken is well covered with the panko. Repeat until all of the chicken has been dipped in all three bowls.

8|

Arrange the chicken tenders on the prepared baking sheet and bake for 25 minutes. Remove from the oven.

9|

Serve the chicken tenders hot with the jalapeño dipping sauce.

Advanced   *50min*   *Meaty*

SPICY DRUMSTICKS WITH EVEN-SPICIER DIPPING SAUCE

This is one of my favorite go-to chicken dishes. It's so simple and great for when you have the munchies, as the spiciness will make you drink a lot!

 6

For the sriracha dipping sauce:

1 cup mayonnaise

¼ cup sriracha sauce

2 tbsp freshly squeezed lemon juice

1 garlic clove, finely minced

1 tsp sweet paprika

Salt, to taste

For the spicy drumsticks:

1 medium red onion

1 habanero stemmed

2 tbsp white wine vinegar

3 cloves garlic

1 tsp rosemary leaves

½ tsp ground cinnamon

Pinch freshly grated nutmeg

½ cup extra-virgin olive oil

½ tsp ground cloves (optional)

Dash liquid smoke (optional, if you're into that)

12 small chicken drumsticks

1|

Make the sriracha dipping sauce: Combine all ingredients in a bowl and stir until well integrated. Season with the salt. Taste and adjust the seasoning as necessary.

2|

Make the spicy drumsticks: In the bowl of a food processor fitted with the "S" blade, combine the onion, habañero, vinegar, garlic, rosemary, cinnamon, nutmeg, and olive oil plus the cloves and liquid smoke, if using, and process until evenly mixed.

3|

Preheat the oven to 400°F. Line a baking sheet with a baking rack or parchment paper.

4|

Transfer the contents of the food processor to a mixing bowl and add the drumsticks. Cover with plastic wrap and set aside to marinate for 25 minutes.

5|

Transfer the drumsticks to the prepared baking sheet and bake for 30 minutes (the rack helps separate the drumsticks from the cooking juices), turning halfway through the cooking time. At the end of the cooking time, turn the oven to broil for another 2 minutes. Remove from the oven.

6|

Serve hot with the sriracha dipping sauce.

Sweet and Savory Apple Salsas

I feel that apple-based salsas don't get the respect they deserve in most kitchens. Apples have it all: they're sweet, tangy, and chewy, and I've seen very few kitchens that don't have a few just sitting in a bowl on the counter. You can't really go wrong if you use the right ingredients—it's just a question of which flavor you'd like to emphasize. To save you the mental exercise, I've presented a couple of options to suit your need.

SAVORY RED & GREEN APPLE SALSA

*After a couple of attempts to prove this thesis of a salsa, I was ready to give up
and chuck this recipe to the archive… but then my dear friend Elena suggested
we boost the salsa's flavor with a clementine, which added the very necessary
moisture that tied it all together.*

1 large green apple peeled and cut into small dice

1 large red apple peeled and cut into small dice

1 medium red onion, finely chopped

1 red bell pepper, seeded and finely chopped

1 clementine peeled and cut into small dice

1 jalapeño pepper, seeded and extra finely chopped

¼ cup finely chopped fresh cilantro

¼ cup finely chopped pistachios or pecans

Freshly squeezed juice of ½ lime

2 tbsp apple cider vinegar

1 tbsp honey

Salt and freshly ground black pepper, to taste

In a large bowl, stir together all the ingredients, season with the salt and black pepper, and set aside for at least 20 minutes. Taste and adjust the seasoning as desired. Serve with some good chips and a cool beer, and enhance it all with a few puffs of your favorite strain.

SWEET GREEN APPLE & NUT SALSA

*Apples, nuts, and red wine are a super combination; once you place all three
together in a dish, it's very hard to screw up.*

4 green apples, peeled and cut into small dice

12 dates, pitted and finely chopped

1 cup chopped walnuts

2 tbsp red wine or brandy

1 tsp freshly grated ginger

Dash ground cinnamon (optional)

½ cup granola (optional)

In a large bowl, stir together all the ingredients, cover with plastic wrap, and refrigerate for at least 1 hour and up to overnight to allow the flavors to meld. This salsa is very "dominant," so I'd suggest serving it with relatively bland chips, lettuce leaves, or a flatbread.

One of the questions I'm most often asked is how I can focus on cooking when I'm high. It's a worthy question, indeed—after all, finely chopping jalapeños, deep-frying tempura, or even trying to spell the word tempura might be unwise while you're flying high up there. So if you're just not much of a planner, or you've started puffing away and then suddenly realized you're about to eat the entire fridge, this chapter is for you. It tries to optimize simplicity with a dash of creativity, all while keeping everything very short and to the point.

06.
While on the High

COOKING ON THE HIGH: THINGS TO REMEMBER

Let's start with an obvious statement: if you're going to cook while on the high, you must have minimal proficiency in both fields. If you've never smoked a joint before and can barely cook rice, I wouldn't advise attempting to combine your first high with a challenging culinary endeavor. It might end up being the best thing you've ever tasted, but also it might leave you with a burnt pan and singed eyebrows.

But if you enjoy cooking and indulge in the occasional high, I find combining the two to be extremely rewarding. In fact, some of my most tasty and fun creations were conceived while under the influence. It heightens my adventurous spirit and allows me to try unorthodox combinations and to challenge various virtual cooking barriers. After all, cooking can be a very creative process, and it often goes beyond a pure mechanical need for sustenance.

It is true that the duo of being high and kitchenware can pose some risks, but if you behave responsibly, you can enjoy the meditative qualities of the practice without a worry. Following are some guidelines to get you started.

GET YOUR ZEN ON AND DON'T MULTITASK

Don't let a false sense of security cloud your judgement. You are going to be spaced out, so cook in a linear fashion, not in parallel. Try to be strategic and plan ahead: don't start sautéing the garlic while you're chopping the chilies, slicing the onions, and peeling the carrots. Get everything in order before you start cooking. Focus on one task at a time, and be mindful. Enjoy it: you're high and you're cooking. That's a privilege.

BE CAREFUL WITH SHARP AND HOT

I know this is self-explanatory, but many of us get complacent and think, "We've got this." Make sure you cook the food and not yourself. Grip hot handles with towels, use lids, and cut slowly and away from your fingers. Wear sturdy shoes in case something sharp falls or a glass breaks. Reduce clutter and put your knives back in their place when you're done. I'll spare you the gory details about times I've sliced my fingers along with my veggies while elevated but take the word of a wounded veteran and be cautious.

LISTEN TO MUSIC

Music and weed are closely tied together. Many of the greatest contemporary creations have come about thanks to a boost in creative powers from marijuana. Music, weed, and cooking combined are just... awesome together. I've discovered many of my favorite tunes while cooking on the high, and I believe that cooking in silence takes away a lot from the experience. So take the time to choose whatever rocks your world and allow it to take you away. An important note before you do: music is great if it's coming from headphones or a speaker, but don't use a screen, as you'll most likely find yourself gazing at it instead of focusing on cooking.

TIMERS ARE YOUR FRIENDS

Time perception is different while on the high, and it's easy to get distracted by virtually anything. I carry significant scar tissue from having burnt, dried out, and forgotten many dishes. If nothing else, learn from my mistakes and use a timer.

BEFORE YOU EAT, DOUBLE CHECK TO MAKE SURE EVERYTHING IS OFF

Make sure you've shut off the gas burners and oven, closed the fridge door, and turned off whatever electrical appliances you've used before you sit down to eat. And once you've made sure, do it again. We all get forgetful, even while sober. Leaving stuff on—especially gas burners—can be extremely dangerous to your health and property. Don't ignore this warning: otherwise, instead of a great recipe, you'll have a recipe for disaster (see what I did there?).

Simple   25min   Vegetarian

OOZY STUFFED SOURDOUGH LOAF FIT FOR ALL LEVELS OF HIGH

The perfect baked good for the baked cook. The required attention span is very minimal and the return very high… or at least seems that way to people who are very high while they're eating it. However, just in case the complexity levels are too high, I've simplified this recipe to accommodate any level of motor skills.

8

1 unsliced loaf sourdough bread

4 oz room-temperature cream cheese

3 stems scallions, finely chopped

3 tbsp unsalted butter, melted

2 garlic cloves, minced

1 tsp chili powder (optional)

10–15 slices cheese (I like to use Monterey Jack and
provolone, but whatever fits your taste will work),
cut into strips

½ cup cooked bacon bits (optional)

I can manage cooking

1|

Preheat the oven to 350°F.

2|

Using a bread knife, make a diagonal cut through
the top of the bread, leaving the bottom of the
crust intact. Repeat across the entire loaf, with
cuts approximately 1 inch apart. Turn the bread 90
degrees and repeat the slices vertically. When you're
done, the loaf should be cross-cut into 1-inch squares.

3|

Spread the cream cheese between the 1-inch slices in
the bread.

4|

In a mixing bowl, combine together the scallions,
butter, and garlic and the chili powder, if using, and
stir until well combined. Drizzle the mixture over the
bread between all the cracks—don't skimp.

5|

Insert the strips of cheese into the cracks in the bread;
the strips should be the same height as the slices in
the bread so they don't stick out of the top of the loaf.

6|

Lay a long piece of foil on the counter horizontally
and a second long piece on top of it vertically. Place
the stuffed bread loaf in the center of the foil 'cross'
and wrap the loaf.

7|

Bake for 15 minutes. Open the top of the foil and
bake for another 5 to 10 minutes, tear the bread apart
and enjoy.

I can manage

Forget the cream cheese. It's not that important;
you'll still enjoy a lovely dish without challenging
yourself too much.

I can?

Forget the melted butter mix (that means no
scallions or garlic as well). Just create a weird
crisscross version of a grilled cheese sandwich. You
won't be left hungry.

I... eh, what were we talking about?!

Just eat the bread. You'll survive. Enjoy the flight...

Simple   15min   Vegetarian

PERSONAL NUKED VEGGIE LASAGNA

When your heart desires comfort, but your attention span is spotty, this fail-safe personal lasagna comes to the rescue!

 1

1–2 dried lasagna noodles (the ones you cook)

Boiling water, as needed

½ cup chopped fresh spinach (optional)

½ cup ricotta cheese (use sour cream if you don't have ricotta)

½ cup shredded mozzarella

¼ medium bell pepper, diced

¼ tsp garlic powder

½ tsp dried basil or thyme

½ cup marinara sauce

¼ cup chopped cooked sausage (optional)

1|

Break the lasagna sheets into quarters and place them in a bowl. Cover the noodles with the boiling water and set aside for 8 minutes (they will soften).

2|

If you're using the spinach, place it in a microwave-safe bowl. Cover the top with plastic wrap and poke a few holes in it. Microwave for 1 minute on high.

3|

In a mixing bowl, combine the ricotta, 3 tbsp of the mozzarella, the bell pepper, the garlic powder, and the basil. If you've decided to add the sausage and/or spinach, add them as well. Mix thoroughly.

4|

Pour half the marinara sauce into the bottom of your cooking mug or bowl. Cover with a third of the noodles. Add ½ of the contents of the mixing bowl and cover with the next third of the noodles. Add the rest of the contents of the mixing bowl and top with the remaining noodles. Add the remaining marinara sauce and sprinkle with the remaining mozzarella.

5|

Microwave for 2 minutes on high. Check to make sure that the mozzarella is melted; if it isn't, continue cooking in 30-second intervals until the cheese is fully melted.

6|

Serve hot.

Hack Your Ramen Bowl

If you're like me, not only have you enjoyed your fair share of instant ramen meals, you've also got a weird affinity for them. I don't know what it is—probably the MSG—but there's something very comforting about a steamy bowl of brothy ramen. But as time has gone by, I've started to think of ramen more as a canvas on which I can explore and paint amazing works of culinary art. I shared four variations here, each of which accommodates different levels of high.

COCONUT CURRY RAMEN
[SOARING ALTITUDE]

1 packet Oriental or chicken flavor instant
    ramen noodles
1 cup light coconut milk
1 tbsp curry powder
1 tsp cayenne powder (optional)

Prepare the instant ramen according to the
instructions but replace 1 cup of the water with the
coconut milk. Cook for 5 minutes. Stir in the curry
powder and, if you so desire, the cayenne powder
and enjoy.

EGG DROP RAMEN NOODLES
[FLYING ALTITUDE]

1 packet chicken flavor instant ramen noodles

Water, to cover

1 whole large egg

2 scallions, stemmed and thinly sliced

1|

In a pot over medium heat, combine the dried ramen noodles and the flavor packet and cover with the water. Cook for 5 minutes, or until it reaches a soft boil and the noodles are pretty much ready.

2|

Carefully break the egg into the broth and cook for an additional 2 minutes—with no stirring, as the egg should stay whole.

3|

Transfer to a serving bowl and top with the sliced scallions for added crunch. Enjoy.

RAMEN WITH SEAWEED AND BOK CHOY
[CLIMBING ALTITUDE]

1 packet Oriental or chicken flavor instant
   ramen noodles
1 small bunch bok choy, roughly sliced
Salt, to taste
2 tbsp nori (dried seaweed), roughly chopped

1|
Prepare the instant ramen according to the instructions.

2|
In a skillet over medium-high heat, place the bok choy (no need for oil). Season with the salt and sauté, stirring constantly, for 1 to 2 minutes, or until the bok choy just starts to wilt. Remove from the heat.

3|
Pour the ramen into a serving bowl. Add the bok choy and nori and serve.

RAMEN WITH STIR-FRIED BEEF
[CRUISING ALTITUDE]

2 packets beef, picante beef, or roast chicken flavor
  instant ramen noodles

2 tbsp vegetable oil

1 lb flank steak, cut into thin strips

1 cup fresh mushrooms, thinly sliced

4 scallions, stemmed and thinly sliced

Salt, to taste

1 cup fresh spinach

1 clove garlic, minced

1–2 tsp chili powder, or to taste

1 tsp minced fresh ginger

¼ cup chopped fresh cilantro, for garnish

1|

Prepare the instant ramen according to the instructions. Once the soup is ready, reduce the heat in order to maintain its temperature.

2|

In a wok over high heat, warm the vegetable oil. Add the steak, mushrooms, and scallions. Lightly season with the salt and cook, stirring frequently, for 3 to 4 minutes, or until the steak looks almost ready.

3|

Add the spinach, garlic, chili powder, and ginger to the wok and continue cooking and stirring for an additional 3 minutes.

4|

Pour a generous portion of the ramen and broth into a serving bowl. Add the contents of the wok and garnish with the cilantro. Serve hot.

Simple   5min   Vegetarian

PIZZA IN A MUG

Get the phone?! Order a delivery?! Wait 30 minutes?!?! Why go to all of that trouble when a perfectly good alternative is sitting in your kitchen, just two minutes away?

 1

4 tbsp all-purpose flour

Pinch baking powder

Pinch baking soda

Pinch salt

3 tbsp milk

1 tbsp olive oil

2 tbsp marinara sauce

3 tbsp shredded mozzarella

Pinch dried Italian herbs or dried oregano

Pepperoni, olives, corn, avocado bits, gorgonzola cheese, or whatever else comes to mind, for topping (optional)

1|

In a microwave-safe mug, stir together the flour, baking powder, baking soda, and salt.

2|

Stir in the milk and oil until the batter reaches an even consistency.

3|

Place the marinara sauce on top of the batter. Using a spoon, gently spread it all around the top of the batter.

4|

Add the cheese, the herbs, and, if using, your choice of the toppings. Microwave on high for 80 seconds.

5|

Devour!

Simple   15min   Vegetarian

BROILED GRAPEFRUIT

The thing I like most about this dish—other than it being one of the simplest and healthiest kitchen hacks ever—is the skeptical looks I get whenever I make it. Of course, once people understand just how awesome this grapefruit twist is, those looks are typically replaced by raised eyebrows and surprised and giddy expressions. I like making this whenever I feel like indulging myself with a morning joint. It's so light that it doesn't weigh me down, yet it fulfills my munch needs.

 2

1 red grapefruit, halved

2 tbsp honey or maple syrup

2 tbsp brown sugar

½ tsp ground cinnamon (optional)

Greek yogurt, for serving

1|

Preheat the oven to 350°F. Line a baking sheet with parchment paper.

2|

Using a small, sharp knife, loosen the sections of grapefruit.

3|

Drizzle the honey or maple syrup on top of the grapefruit halves and generously sprinkle them with the brown sugar and, if using, the cinnamon.

4|

Bake for 12 minutes, or until the grapefruit's top has formed a soft, caramelized crust.

5|

Serve hot with the Greek yogurt and some of the scrapings from the parchment paper on the baking tray.

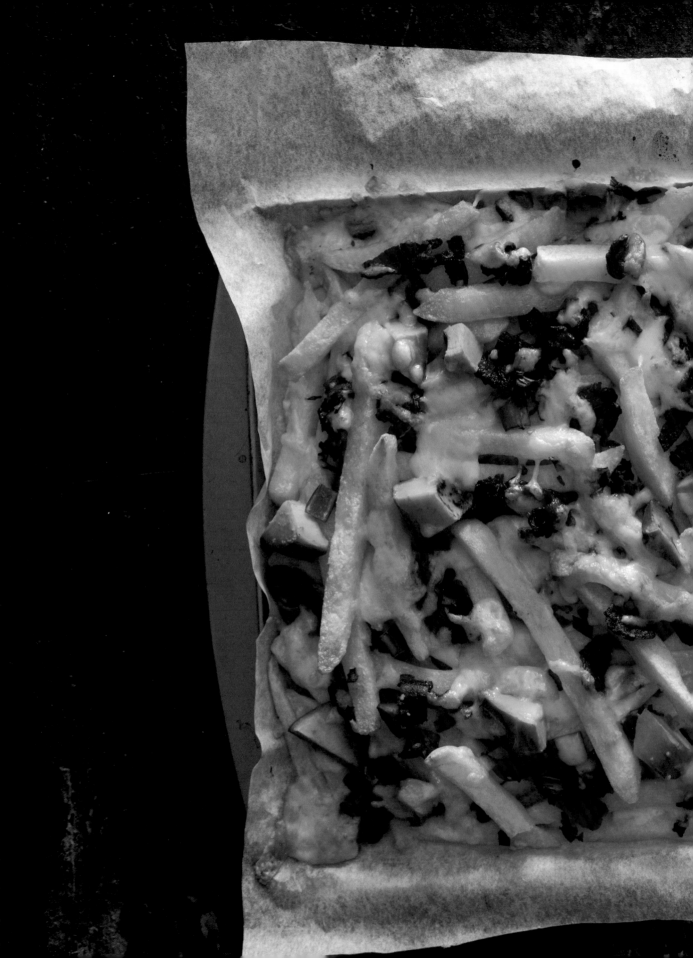

Supercharged French Fries

Frozen French fries are just so... ordinary. Why not take them up a notch with some creative twists? A few minutes of work can be really rewarding.

TRUFFLE FRIES

I love truffles, and with just a pinch of truffle-infused salt or olive oil sprinkled over fries once they're hot out of the oven, you can instantly upgrade your experience. If you have the energy and the attention span, you can also create a quick truffle aioli for dipping by combining ½ cup mayonnaise, ½ cup sour cream, 1 minced garlic clove, 1 tbsp white truffle oil, and salt.

GARLIC, PARMESAN & HERBS

In a small mixing bowl, stir together a few minced garlic cloves, some Parmesan cheese, and some dried thyme or oregano or—if you're up for it—chopped fresh chives or parsley. Mix well with the fries right after they come out of the oven.

MAKE 'EM GREEK

Place fries in a mixing bowl and add 2 tsp of olive oil. Season with a pinch of garlic powder and oregano and some salt and black pepper and toss well. Bake until golden. Remove from the oven and generously add crumbled feta cheese. Return to the oven for an additional 5 minutes. Drizzle with some freshly squeezed lemon juice and serve with Tzatziki (see p. 158) as a great addition.

LOADED TACO FRIES

Place the French fries on a baking sheet and prepare them according to the instructions but for only half the specified baking time. Remove from the oven and top the fries with shredded cheese and chopped cooked bacon, green onions, jalapeño peppers, and avocado. Return to the oven and complete the full baking time. Remove from the oven, add a generous serving of sour cream, and eat up.

INSTANT POUTINE-LIKE FRIES

Poutine is a quintessentially Canadian concoction of fries, gravy, and cheese curds. Since we're making a near-instant 'high-appropriate' version of it, I took the liberty of making a few shortcuts.

Spread out the frozen fries on a baking sheet and generously sprinkle a few chunks of mozzarella cheese on top (don't use shredded mozzarella, as it'll melt completely). Bake the fries for the recommended baking time, and while they're baking, melt 1 tbsp unsalted butter in a skillet over medium heat. Once the butter is melted, add 1 tbsp all-purpose flour and ½ cup beef broth. Stir until the mixture has an even consistency. Cook for another minute or two, or until the gravy thickens. Remove from the heat and season with salt and black pepper. When the fries are done—and while they're still hot—transfer them to a bowl and drizzle the gravy over them. Top with chopped jalapeño peppers and green onions and dig in.

Simple   *5min*   *Vegetarian*

BABY CAPRESE NIBBLES

A super-easy, healthy, and tasty little munch.

 10

20 large, firm cherry tomatoes

6 oz high-quality feta cheese or 20 bocconcini
(mini mozzarella balls)

20 toothpicks

20 small fresh basil leaves

¼ cup olive oil

3 tbsp + 1 tsp aged balsamic vinegar (the very best
you can find)

1 tbsp sea salt

1|

Cut a small slice off the bottom of each cherry
tomato so that they can sit flat on a platter.

2|

Divide the feta into 20 equal pieces (the bocconcini
are an even easier choice!).

3|

Skewer the cherry tomatoes with the toothpicks, flat
side facing down. Stand the tomatoes on a serving
platter. Add a basil leaf to each skewer and top each
with a piece of the cheese.

4|

Generously sprinkle the olive oil and balsamic vinegar
over the skewers and season with the salt. Enjoy!

Simple   15min   Vegan

WHYTAI'S AWESOME POPCORN RECIPE

Popcorn is the ultimate high munch- it's easy to make, it's tasty, it's healthy, and you can chew on it for hours. The big problem is making it come out perfect every time. Sure, you can buy it pre-popped in a bag, but that just doesn't compare with making a fresh batch yourself—and neither do the microwave versions. Luckily, my close friend WhyTai took it upon himself to research the matter. Being the crazy engineer that he is, WhyTai got it down to the perfect formula. He was kind enough to share his trial and error process with me and gift us all with his wisdom. We thank him for that.

Tip: If you have a pot with a clear lid, use it. Leaning over a clear lid and watching the corn kernels pop in real time is a favorite high-times activity.
Another tip: Instead of regular salt, use truffle salt. It will generously reward your taste buds with an upgraded twist.

Deep pot with a lid (hopefully a clear one)
Canola oil
Popcorn kernels
Salt, to taste
1 ready empty bowl
Melted salted butter (optional)

1|
Cover the bottom of a deep pot with a thin layer of the canola oil. While the oil is still cold, add the popcorn kernels until a single layer covers the bottom of the pot. Sprinkle generously with the salt.

2|
Place over medium heat. As the oil begins to heat up and thins, grab the pot and gently shake it to make sure all the kernels are warming equally.

3|
As soon as the first kernel pops, quickly cover the pot. After a minute or so, the popping will become very

frequent. Keep the pot covered and shake it gently every 20 seconds during the cooking time.

4|
Listen carefully: once the popping rate decreases to a pop every 3 seconds, immediately remove from the heat and transfer the popcorn to a bowl—otherwise, it might burn.

5|
Taste and season again with the salt and/or the salted butter. Stir well and eat while hot.

Simple   *20min*   *Vegetarian*

SWEET CAMOUFLAGED PRETZEL STICKS

This is one of the sweet, fun treats I enjoy making most while on the high.
It's really simple—so simple that even the highest among us all will find they
can rise to the challenge.

 10

3½ oz (100g) dark chocolate, broken into
medium pieces

3½ oz (100g) semi-sweet chocolate, broken
into medium pieces

30 long pretzel sticks (I prefer the ones that
are generously sprinkled with sea salt)

Crushed nuts, sprinkles, coconut flakes, or
crushed cookies, for garnish

1|

Line a baking sheet with parchment paper.

2|

Place the chocolate pieces in a microwave-safe
bowl and microwave in 20-second intervals on high;
between each interval, stir well until the chocolate
has fully melted.

3|

Transfer the melted chocolate to a tall glass and dip
each pretzel in it until the pretzel is 7/8 covered.

4|

Arrange your garnish choices on small plates. While
the chocolate is still soft, roll the pretzel sticks in the
garnish/es. Transfer the sticks to the prepared baking
sheet to rest until the chocolate becomes solid.
(For accelerated results, place the baking sheet in
the fridge.)

5|

Dig in!

Simple   *20min*   *Vegetarian*

RAM 'N' CHEESE

This classic-with-a-twist allows the high cook quicker gratification and a guaranteed satisfactory outcome. I've known people who tried this recipe and never went back to old-school mac 'n' cheese again. Just saying…

2

2 packages ramen noodles (without the flavor
  packets)
1 tbsp canola oil
1-2 tbsp unsalted butter
1 tbsp flour

¾ cup milk, plus more as needed
1 cup grated mild Cheddar cheese
¼ cup crumbled goat cheese, for sprinkling
¼ cup roasted pine nuts, for sprinkling

1|

Bring a pot of water to a boil. Add the ramen noodles
and cook for 2 minutes (no more than that, as it'll get
too mushy). Remove from the heat and drain into a
colander. Rinse the noodles with cold water.

2|

Transfer the noodles to a bowl and add the canola oil.
Toss them thoroughly with your hands, taking care to
break up any lumps and evenly coat the noodles with
the oil.

3|

In a large saucepan over medium heat, warm the
butter. Add the flour to the saucepan and stir
until combined.

4|

Add the milk to the saucepan and cook, stirring
constantly with a wooden spoon, until it reaches a
thick consistency.

5|

Add the Cheddar cheese and noodles to the pan and
cook, stirring constantly, for 2 minutes. If you are
seeking a looser consistency, add more milk. Remove
from the heat.

6|

Transfer to a bowl. Sprinkle the goat cheese and pine
nuts over the mixture and serve.

The whole notion of investing two minutes to mix something in a cup and then ninety seconds later enjoying a great cake never fails to delight me.

Three Cakes in a Cup

GOOEY ZAPPED COOKIES 'N' CREAM
CAKE IN A MUG

¼ cup semisweet chocolate chips

3 tbsp whole milk

¼ cup all-purpose flour

2 Oreo cookies, crushed, plus more for serving

¼ tbsp vegetable oil

¼ tsp baking powder

¼ tsp vanilla extract

Schlag (see p. 236), for serving (optional)

1| In a microwave-safe bowl or mug, combine the chocolate chips and milk. Microwave in 20-second intervals; between each interval, stir until the chocolate is melted and uniform. Make sure to not overheat the chocolate, as it burns easily.

2| Add the remaining ingredients and stir until the batter is smooth and consistent.

3| Microwave on high for 70 seconds.

4| Top with more of the crushed Oreos and the Schlag and serve.

NUKED HAZELNUT AND CHOCOLATE JUG

4 tbsp all-purpose flour

3 tbsp confectioners' sugar

2 tbsp cocoa powder

1 tsp vanilla extract

½ tsp baking powder

3 tbsp heavy cream

1 tbsp vegetable oil

1 tbsp Nutella spread

2 tbsp crushed hazelnuts

1| Combine the flour, sugar, cocoa powder, vanilla extract and baking powder in a microwave-safe mug.

2| Gradually whisk in the cream and oil until the batter is smooth.

3| Drop the Nutella into the middle of the batter. Top with the hazelnuts.

4| Microwave on high for 80 seconds, or until the cake looks firm.

5| Serve hot.

MICROWAVE CARROT CAKE WITH MAPLE AND VANILLA GLAZE

For the cake:

¼ cup all-purpose flour

1 tbsp confectioners' sugar

½ tsp ground cinnamon

¼ tsp baking powder

Dash salt

1 tbsp milk

1 tbsp vegetable oil

1 carrot, peeled and grated

For the maple-vanilla glaze:

4 tbsp confectioners' sugar

1 tbsp unsalted butter, melted

1 tsp good maple syrup

¼ tsp vanilla extract

1 tbsp heavy cream (if you don't have cream, you can use milk)

1| Make the cake: Combine the flour, sugar, cinnamon, baking powder, and salt in a microwave-safe mug.

2| Gradually stir in the milk and oil. Add the carrot and stir well.

3| Microwave on high for 90 seconds.

4| Make the glaze: Stir together all the ingredients except the cream. Start to whisk the mixture and, while whisking constantly, gradually add the cream. Continue whisking until you reach you the desired consistency of the glaze.

5| Spoon the glaze over the carrot mug cake while it's hot. Set aside for 2 minutes to allow the glaze to soak in.

6| Serve warm.

When I started writing this book, I found that this chapter was the one that was most frequently challenged by my readers. It wasn't that my smoking comrades weren't into eating healthy—instead, I was confronted with an overall sentiment that the sporadic habit of weed consumption was correlated with a more substantial habit of eating junk.

I find this isn't the case. On the contrary: I know many people who regret their binge munchies and consider it a drawback of their weed experience. For those people, I say fear not! This chapter is here for you. Feeling high and eating food with a high nutritional content are tightly connected; they're good for both your mind and your body.

07.
Healthy and Satisfying

Make-It-Your-Own Lettuce Wrap Station

There is a clear difference between eating and munching. The best munchies are healthy, don't weigh you down, and can be enjoyed for a couple of hours. This is one of the best: it keeps everyone engaged and allows you to build whatever combination you desire. I used to do this with taco shells (and you can certainly go for that option as well), but lettuce and cabbage leaves turned out to be better choices.

In addition to the suggestions I include here, I typically add a few bowls with grated cheese, finely chopped jalapeños, cilantro and potentially some other toppings, depending on the mood and availability... I'll leave this part to your imagination

CHIPOTLE-STYLE CHICKEN AND SWEET POTATOES

For the marinade:

½ red onion, peeled

½ cup water

4 cloves garlic, peeled

2 tbsp extra-virgin olive oil

1 tbsp freshly squeezed lime juice

1 tsp chipotle chili powder

1 tsp chili powder

½ tsp ground cumin

½ tsp smoked paprika

½ tsp salt

½ tsp freshly ground black pepper

For the chicken and sweet potatoes:

3 tbsp extra-virgin olive oil

2 large chicken breasts, pounded thin

2 large sweet potatoes, peeled and diced extra small

Salt, to taste

Sweet paprika, to taste

3 large scallions, finely chopped

1|

Make the marinade: In the jug of a blender, combine all of the marinade ingredients and puree until smooth. You should smell the chipotle aroma as it blends. Set aside a third of the marinade for later use.

2|

Make the chicken: Cut a few slices in the tops of the chicken breasts. In a large zip-top bag, combine the remaining contents of the blender and the chicken breasts and refrigerate for 1½ hours.

3|

In a skillet over medium heat, warm the olive oil. Add the sweet potato and stir fry until they take on a beautiful golden and charred look (the sweet potato pieces must be very small, or this will take a long time and the oil might burn).

4|

Add the set-aside third of the marinade to the skillet and season with the salt and paprika. Sauté for 3 minutes, or until the spices have coated all the sweet potato.

5|

Grill the chicken on medium-high heat for 5 to 6 minutes per side (alternately, you can cook them with 2 tbsp of olive oil in a very hot, heavy-bottomed skillet).

6|

Move the grilled chicken breasts to a cutting board and set aside for 5 minutes to allow the juices to redistribute.

7|

Chop the chicken into slices and transfer to a serving bowl. Toss in the sweet potatoes and scallions and mix well.

HONEY SESAME BEEF WITH CORN AND BROCCOLI

¼ cup soy sauce

¼ cup honey

2 tbsp ketchup

2 cloves garlic, minced

1 tsp fresh ginger, peeled and minced

¼ cup warm water

1 tsp cornstarch

2 tbsp canola oil

1 lb skirt steak, thinly sliced and at room temperature

1 cup broccoli florets, finely chopped

Kernels from 1 fresh ear corn

4 scallions, finely chopped, for garnish

2 tbsp sesame seeds, for garnish

1|

In a small bowl, whisk together the soy sauce, honey, ketchup, garlic, and ginger. In a separate bowl, whisk together the warm water and cornstarch.

2|

In a large skillet over medium heat, warm the canola oil. Add the steak slices, broccoli, and corn and sauté, stirring constantly, for 6 minutes, or until the beef is cooked through.

3|

Add the contents of the first bowl to the skillet, reduce the heat to low, and cook for an additional 2 minutes. Stir in the cornstarch slurry until the mixture thickens and remove from heat.

4|

Serve garnished with the scallions and sesame seeds.

COCONUT CURRIED CAULIFLOWER COUSCOUS WITH CABBAGE TORTILLAS

1 large head cauliflower, cut into 1-inch florets

3 tbsp canola oil

2 large carrots, peeled and finely chopped

1 large zucchini, finely chopped

Salt and freshly ground black pepper, to taste

2 cups light coconut milk

Freshly squeezed juice of ½ lemon

2 tsp curry powder

1 tsp chili flakes

¼ cup finely chopped cashews

Whole leaves of 1 large cabbage, for serving

1 small (8-oz) container sour cream, for serving

1|

Coarsely grate the cauliflower florets. The texture should resemble uncooked rice.

2|

In a large skillet over medium heat, warm the canola oil. Add the carrots and stir-fry, stirring constantly, for 8 minutes, or until the carrots turn golden.

3|

Add the zucchini and cauliflower to the skillet and season with the salt and black pepper. Continue cooking, stirring constantly, for 3 to 5 minutes.

4|

Reduce the heat to low and add the coconut milk, lemon juice, curry powder, and chili flakes. Simmer for 10 minutes. Remove from the heat.

5|

Transfer the contents of the skillet to a serving bowl. Sprinkle on the cashews—this is very important, as they add a necessary crunch.

6|

Place a generous spoonful of the mixture on a cabbage leaf. Add another generous spoonful of the sour cream and devour.

Advanced   *20min*   *Meaty*

AHI TUNA AND DRIED FRUIT POKE BOWL

This one's for the sushi lovers: a next-gen alternative that's both easier to make (very handy when on the high) and, if you ask me, tastier to consume.

 6

For the relish:

8 Medjool dates, pitted and finely chopped

¼ cup + 2 tbsp soy sauce

¼ cup water

1 tbsp freshly grated ginger

1 tbsp freshly grated orange zest

2 tbsp finely chopped fresh chives, for garnish

For the poke bowl:

20 oz ahi tuna steaks (approx. 3–4 steaks)

1 tbsp olive oil

1 tbsp white and/or black sesame seeds

2 cups cooked rice (white or brown)

Salt and freshly ground black pepper, to taste

1|

Make the relish: In a mixing bowl, combine the dates, soy sauce, water, ginger and orange zest. Garnish with the chives. Set aside.

2|

Make the poke: In a heavy skillet over high heat, warm the olive oil carefully, making sure it doesn't burn.

3|

Season the ahi tuna steaks with the salt and black pepper. Add the steaks to the skillet and sear to the desired level of doneness on each side. Remove from the heat.

4|

Transfer the steaks to a cutting board and cut them into thin slices.

5|

To a wide, rectangular serving plate, add equal portions of the rice and slices of the tuna. Top each with a teaspoon of the relish and serve.

Simple   15min   Vegetarian

BIG G. SCRAPPY SALAD

Once, after a very welcome surprise visit by some old friends and neighbors, we found ourselves sitting for hours and reminiscing about old times. Before long, as with all friendly encounters, requests for nourishment arose.
I opened my fridge and took out whatever I had to make this scrappy salad. Appeals for a re-do have kept coming since, and if there's one thing I've learned about cooking, it's this: if the people want it, give it to them. So in the spirit of sharing the love, here's the recipe for a tasty, healthy salad made from the random ingredients I had in my fridge that evening.

 4

1 cup thickly sliced cherry tomatoes

3 radishes, thinly sliced

1 red pepper, finely chopped

1 jalapeño pepper, seeded and super finely chopped

3 scallions, finely chopped

1 small bunch fresh flat-leaf parsley, finely chopped

⅓ cup pine nuts

½ cup excellent-quality feta cheese, cubed

2 tbsp extra-virgin olive oil

Freshly squeezed juice of 1 small lemon

Salt and freshly ground black pepper, to taste

1 tbsp za'atar seasoning (optional but highly
   recommended)

1 fresh loaf sourdough bread, sliced, for serving

Tzatziki (see p. 158), for serving

1|

In a large salad bowl, combine all the chopped vegetables.

2|

In a small dry skillet over high heat, roast the pine nuts for 2 to 3 minutes (roasted pine nuts are crunchy and delicious, but they burn quickly—be careful not to blacken them). Remove from the heat.

3|

Add the pine nuts, cheese, lemon juice, and olive oil, as well as the za'atar, if using, to the vegetables and toss well.

4|

Serve with the tzatziki and sourdough bread.

A ninja bowl is great for long seatings—times when you fear you may end up binging excessively. It can be enjoyed at room temperature, and there's absolutely no need to make it on the spot. My recommendation is to prep this just as you're getting started, so it'll be available for the hours to come.

Ninja Quinoa Bowl with Your Choice of Dressings

THE BASIC BOWL

3 cups cooked quinoa (approx. 1 cup uncooked)

2 medium sweet potatoes, diced

1 small head cauliflower, cut into bite-size florets

1 small head broccoli, cut into bite-size florets

Extra-virgin olive oil

Salt and freshly ground black pepper, to taste

½ head green cabbage, shredded

½ head red cabbage, shredded

1 small bunch fresh cilantro, chopped

½ cup chopped scallions

½ cup broken pistachios

1|

Preheat the oven to 350°F.

2|

Arrange the sweet potatoes, cauliflower and broccoli florets on a baking sheet and sprinkle generously with the olive oil, salt, and black pepper. Bake for 35 to 40 minutes, stirring after the first 20 minutes of cooking time. Remove from the oven.

3|

While the vegetables are in the oven, prepare your choice of the three ninja dressing options that follow.

4|

Now to plate the dish – combine the grilled vegetables with the red and green cabbage and scallions. Ask yourself which camp you belong to: are you one of those people who sets up each ingredient separately in the bowl, or do you mix it all up and serve it stirred, but not shaken? There's no wrong answer, by the way, it's just a matter of some culinary je ne sais quoi. Assemble your bowl how you like it, sprinkle pistachios on top and enjoy.

THE MEDITERRANEAN NINJA DRESSING

Freshly squeezed juice of 1 lemon

3 tbsp extra-virgin olive oil

1 clove garlic, minced

Salt and freshly ground black pepper, to taste

1 tsp za'atar seasoning (optional but recommended)

2–3 tbsp Green Tahini (see p. 162; optional but
   highly recommended)

In a small bowl, whisk together the lemon juice, olive oil, and garlic until it reaches an even consistency. Season with the salt and black pepper. Whisk in the optional ingredients as desired to customize the dressing to your tastes.

SESAME-GARLIC NINJA DRESSING

3 tbsp soy sauce

2 tbsp honey

2 tbsp rice vinegar

2 tbsp warm water

Freshly squeezed juice of ½ lime

1 tbsp sesame oil

2 garlic cloves, minced

1 (½-inch) piece ginger root, peeled and freshly grated

In a small bowl, whisk together all the ingredients.

LEMON VINAIGRETTE NINJA DRESSING

½ cup extra-virgin olive oil

¼ cup red wine vinegar

Freshly squeezed juice of 1 lemon

2 tbsp dried oregano

2 tbsp Dijon mustard

1 tbsp honey

1 clove garlic, finely minced

1 tsp salt

¼ tsp freshly ground black pepper

In a small bowl, whisk together all the ingredients.

Moderate   20min   Vegan

MUSSABACHA

You might be wondering what's up with this weird name. Well, Mussabacha originates from the Arabic word for "morning." This heavy and tasty dish is served for breakfast in some Middle Eastern cuisines. This recipe definitely has its pros and cons: it does take time to prep everything, but after a bit of work, you're all set with an awesome dish for the next few times you venture into the highland.

 2

½ cup small dried garbanzo beans*

Lots of water

1 tsp baking soda

¼ cup + 1 tbsp Plain Ole Tahini (see p. 162)

Freshly squeezed juice of 1 lemon, plus more as desired

1 tbsp extra-virgin olive oil, plus more as desired

½ tsp ground cumin, plus more as desired

Salt and freshly ground black pepper, to taste

1 tomato, chopped

1 small onion, super finely chopped

1 small bunch fresh flat-leaf parsley leaves, finely chopped

3 tbsp pine nuts

1 tsp sweet paprika

Because dried garbanzo beans have to be soaked overnight and cooked for hours, I recommend preparing 2–3 cups of them at a time and then freezing what you don't use for future consumption.

** You can use canned beans if you'd like. It will still taste good; just make sure to rinse them well in a colander. Replace the cooking water with half a cup of warm water and skip to step 3.

1|

In a deep bowl, cover the garbanzo beans with water and soak overnight.** They will expand in volume, so make sure to use plenty of water.

2|

Drain the beans and transfer the garbanzo beans to a deep pot. Cover again with fresh water, add the baking soda and cook over low heat for 3 hours, or until the beans are very soft. Remove from the heat. Drain, retaining ¼ cup of the cooking water.

3|

Transfer the beans and cooking water to a pan over low heat. Add the tahini and simmer for 3 minutes (this will give it more of a porridge texture). Remove from the heat.

4|

Transfer the beans to a large serving bowl. Add the lemon juice, olive oil, and cumin and season with the salt and black pepper. Toss until well combined. Taste and adjust the seasoning as desired.

5|

Top with the tomato, onion, and parsley. Garnish with the pine nuts and paprika and serve.

Moderate   6-18h   Vegan

HOMEMADE DRIED FRUIT

This is one of the tastiest, healthiest, and most satisfying recipes I know.
Who knew that a single apple could be "translated" into an hour of light
munching. Once they're dried, they're sweet and chewy, and this is so easy to
make—a no brainer!

1 or more ripe but not-too-ripe apple, peach,
    strawberry, apricot, mango, pineapple, or plum

1|

Preheat the oven to 150°F. Line a baking sheet with a
rack or parchment paper.

2|

If using a pineapple or mango, peel the fruit. Remove
and discard any cores, pits, and stems.

3|

Thoroughly rinse the fruit and dry it well using a
kitchen towel, taking care that no lint or paper sticks
to the fruit.

4|

Cut the fruit into thin, but not razor-thin, slices.
Remember: the slices will shrivel up by at least half
their size.

5|

Evenly spread the fruit slices on the rack or the
prepared baking sheet, making sure that none of the
slices touch each other.

6|

Bake the fruit for 6 to 18 hours, making sure to flip
over the slices every few hours. The baking time
depends on the type of fruit used, the width of the
slices, and desired level of crunch. Remove from
the oven.

7|

Ideally, the dried fruit should be stored at room
temperature for 1 day before consuming, but if you
don't have the time, feel free to eat it immediately
and let the next bunch wait.

8|

Store in a sealed container at room temperature for
up to 4 months.

Moderate *2h* *Vegan*

JUST CAULIFLOWER

I love this dish: you put in five minutes of work and throw it in the oven. After a couple of hours, just when your stomach starts signaling that it's ready for munchies consumption, you simply pull it out of the oven, tear the foil, and dig in. If you're in the right state of mind to walk the extra mile, I'd advise boiling some water in a deep pot and dunking the cauliflower for 2 minutes (and no longer) before wrapping it in the foil. This gives the cauliflower extra softness.

 4

Lots of aluminum foil

1 whole large head cauliflower, stem removed
 and discarded

1 tomato, finely chopped

¼ cup olive oil

1 tsp sweet paprika

½ tsp ground cumin

Salt and freshly ground black pepper, to taste

1|

Preheat the oven to 350°F. Place a long sheet of foil on the counter.

2|

Place the cauliflower in the center of the foil with the bottom facing up. Place the chopped tomato inside. Invert the head of cauliflower, making sure the tomato bits stay inside. Massage the cauliflower with the olive oil and season with the paprika, cumin, salt, and black pepper.

3|

Wrap the cauliflower three times in the foil. Use as many sheets as necessary and make sure 3 good layers surround the cauliflower. Bake for 2 hours. Remove from the oven.

4|

Rip open the top of the aluminum foil and, if you prefer a charred texture, return it to the oven under the broiler for a few minutes.

5|

Get a bunch of spoons and enjoy.

Simple   3h   Vegetarian

BERRY TASTY MOUSSE

This healthy and refreshing treat is perfect for those times when you can really use a sugar recharge, yet you wish to avoid a chocolate-centric dish. For you visionaries out there, I'd recommend prepping this a few hours in advance, but even if you refrigerate it for only a couple of hours, you'll still enjoy a softened version of the mousse—and that might be enough for the culinary threshold of a high eater.

 4

3 cups assorted berries (I like to use strawberries, blackberries, blueberries, and raspberries)
¼ cup water
1 tbsp superfine sugar

1 cup heavy cream
10 fresh mint leaves, finely chopped
Freshly squeezed juice of ½ lemon

1|

Place the stainless-steel mixing bowl of a stand mixer in the freezer for 10 to 20 minutes.

2|

In the jug of a blender or the bowl of a food processor fitted with the "S" blade, combine 2 cups of the berries, the water, and the sugar and blend till smooth.

3|

Using a stand mixer fitted with the whisk attachment and the chilled bowl, beat the heavy cream on high speed until it becomes stable and fluffy whipped cream. Make sure to not overmix, as it may deflate.

4|

Gently fold the berry puree into the whipped cream just until the color blends evenly.

5|

Fill a small serving bowl or a cup three-quarters of the way full with the berry mousse. Repeat until all of the servings have been made. Cover with plastic wrap and refrigerate for at least 3 hours or overnight (overnight is best).

6|

Before serving, combine the remaining 1 cup berries with the lemon juice and mint leaves. Using a tablespoon, add equal amounts of the mixture to each serving of the mousse.

Simple   20min   Vegetarian

VANILLA FRUIT PARFAIT

*One of the best dishes for munching while high, the vanilla fruit parfait is
great not only because it's cold, sweet, and filling, but also because after
just a few minutes of work, you'll have a phenomenal munch that will keep
everyone happy. You can either make it on the spot or ahead of time; if you
do make ahead, omit the granola, as it will get soggy (you can always add it
when you start eating).*

 4

1 cup excellent-quality granola (add just before eating
   if not consuming right away)

3 cups vanilla yogurt

1 cup chopped mixed fresh fruit (pineapple, mango,
   blueberries, blackberries, and raspberries)

1 cup finely chopped fresh strawberries

Good-quality honey, for drizzling

2 tbsp chia seeds (optional)

1|

Fill each serving bowl or cup with the granola until it
is about a fifth full. Using a spoon, pack the granola
down in the bottom of the bowl. Add an equal
amount of the yogurt.

2|

Add a layer of the mixed fruit and strawberries on top
of the yogurt. Then add another layer of yogurt, and
then another layer of mixed fruit and strawberries.

3|

Drizzle the honey over the top of the parfait and if
you wish to have a thicker consistency to the yogurt,
add the chia seeds.

4|

Serve immediately.

Whether cheesy nachos are your idea of a healthy breakfast or you're just craving a small, light-hearted deviation from an otherwise kale-focused diet, I feel we all need to pamper ourselves with tasty, nutritionally indifferent delights every so often. This chapter is all about comfort. Use these recipes for those sessions when you want to accentuate the de-stressing effect of weed by indulging in a worry-free guilty pleasure.

08.
For the
Nutritionally
Indifferent

Moderate   20min   Vegetarian

NUTELLA-STUFFED FRENCH TOAST WITH HOMEMADE SCHLAG

This guilty pleasure full of sweet goodness will lift everyone's spirits—guaranteed! I first made this recipe when hiking to a remote cabin with a bunch of friends. I sneaked the heavy cream in my bag and transformed what was supposed to be Nutella sandwiches and scrambled eggs into this mouthwatering adventure.

4

4 whole large eggs

¼ cup whole milk

1 loaf French brioche or challah bread

⅓ cup Nutella spread

2 tbsp crushed meringue (optional)

1 tbsp unsalted butter

1 cup heavy whipping cream (highest fat content)

⅓ cup confectioners' sugar

1 tsp vanilla extract

Fresh fruit, for serving

1|

Place a stainless-steel mixing bowl in the freezer for 20 minutes (a good Schlag needs extreme cold).

2|

In a separate mixing bowl, whisk together the eggs and milk until the mixture is even and fluffy. Set aside.

3|

Remove the 2 ends from the loaf of bread and nibble on them while you prepare this recipe. Cut the loaf into 6 thick pieces. Very delicately cut each thick slice in half, but leave one of the sides connected (so each slice will look like a Pac-Man if you slightly open it).

4|

Generously spread the Nutella spread between the slices, and if you're that type of person, add the crushed meringue.

5|

In a skillet over medium heat, warm the butter. Coat the pan evenly with the melted butter and reduce the heat to the lowest setting (since the bread slices are thick, if the heat is too high, it'll sear the outsides of the bread and leave the insides raw).

6|

Dip 1 of the Nutella-stuffed bread slices into the egg mixture, taking care to coat the slice evenly. It's important to quickly dip the bread in the egg mixture, as it will start to dissolve fast (it's best to use your hands).

7|

Once the bread is soaked, quickly shake off any excess egg mixture and place into the hot skillet. Fry the bread slices on each side for roughly 7 minutes. Remove to a platter. Repeat steps 6 and 7 until all the slices have been fried, and then remove from the heat.

8|

Add the whipping cream to the cold mixing bowl and whip on medium-high speed for 3 minutes. After the whipped cream's volume grows and becomes airy, add the confectioners' sugar and vanilla extract and mix on high for another 3 minutes, or until the whipped cream has reached a solid consistency. Make sure not to over-whip, as it may break down.

9|

Serve with the fresh fruit and the whipped cream (Schlag). I always leave some Schlag for the coffee… why not, right?

Moderate   *20min*   *Vegetarian* *

NAAMA'S LITTLE CHAT WITH THE DEVIL

As much as I'd love to take credit for this guilty pleasure, I cannot. While working on this book and shooting photos for the Oozy Stuffed Loaf recipe (see p. 178), our amazing food stylist, Naama, asked "Why not make a sweet version of this one?" This immediately sparked a lively debate that ended up with this perfect twist for the high eater. Don't skip the berry syrup, as its tanginess brings perfect balance to this sugar bomb. For you first timers… I envy you for your experience.

 8

1 loaf sourdough bread, unsliced

3½ oz (100g) dark chocolate

3½ oz (100g) semi-sweet chocolate

3½ oz (100g) white chocolate

20 mini marshmallows

2 cups assorted berries (it's best to use a combination of strawberries, raspberries, and blackberries)

3 tbsp water

1 tbsp refined sugar

1|

Preheat the oven to 350°F.

2|

Using a bread knife, make a diagonal cut through the top of the bread, leaving the bottom of the crust intact. Repeat across the entire loaf, with cuts approximately one inch apart. Turn the bread 90 degrees and repeat the slices vertically. When you're done, the loaf should be cross-cut into 1-inch squares.

3|

Break up the chocolate into pieces. Insert the chocolate pieces and mini marshmallows into the slices in the bread.

4|

Lay a long piece of foil on the counter horizontally, and a second longer piece of foil on top of it vertically. Place the stuffed bread loaf in the center of the foil "cross" and wrap the loaf.

5|

Bake for 15 minutes. Open the top of the foil and bake for another 5 to 10 minutes, or until the chocolate and marshmallows are completely melted. Remove from the oven.

6|

In the jug of a blender, combine the berries, water, and sugar and puree until smooth. If you prefer a silkier texture, run the mixture through a strainer. Generously pour the berry mixture over the bread. Tear off a gooey bread chunk and indulge.

Contains gelatin.

Advanced *40min* *Vegetarian*

GUILTY WHOLE ONION

This is the answer, and the question is less important. Occasionally, I reset my comfort-food meter and go for the guilty onion. And let me tell you: this recipe, when it's hot and served with the right dipping sauce, is one of the most perfect, indulgent culinary treats ever made on earth. The only downside, really, is the quasi-aggressive behavior I exhibit when I realize my friends are expecting me to share.

 4

1 extra-large sweet onion

1 cup whole milk

2 whole large eggs

1 tbsp mayonnaise

1½ cups all-purpose flour

2 tsp salt

2 tsp cayenne pepper

1 tsp garlic powder

1 tsp ground black pepper

¼ tsp dried oregano

¼ tsp dried thyme

Enough vegetable oil to completely cover the onion in the pot

Bacon bits and grated Cheddar cheese (optional)

Wasabi (see p. 148) or jalapeño (see p. 167) dipping sauce, for serving

1|

Slicing the onion is an important, and delicate, process. First, remove the skin without harming the onion. Place the onion down, with the root on the bottom, and, using a sharp knife, cut through the center, creating flower-like petals. For large onions, it's best to make anywhere between 8 and 12 cuts. Make sure to cut almost all the way to the bottom of the onion, because you want the onion to open like a flower.

2|

Place the onion upside down (base up) in a bowl of icy water for 20 to 30 minutes. This will make it easier to separate the onion layers and will allow the batter to seep between them. Remove the onion from the ice water and set it aside to dry for 5 minutes.

3|

In a mixing bowl, beat together the milk, eggs, and mayonnaise.

4|

In a separate bowl, sift together all the dry ingredients: the flour, salt, cayenne pepper, garlic powder, black pepper, oregano, and thyme.

5|

Place the onion in the bowl containing the dry ingredients and, using a spoon (or your hands), coat as much of the onion as you can.

6|

Remove the onion from the dry mixture and gently pat it dry, removing any excess coating. Place the onion in the bowl containing the milk mixture. Again, use a spoon (or your hands) to insert the wet mixture into as many parts of the onion as possible.

7|

Remove the onion from the wet mixture and set it aside to rest for 2 minutes, which allows the batter to stick better. Repeat steps 6 and 7 a second time, and if you're really feeling adventurous, repeat it a third time.

8|

In a small but deep pot (deep enough to completely cover the onion in oil) over medium-high heat, warm the oil to 375°F (if you don't have a thermometer, drizzle a single drop of water into the hot oil and wait until it sizzles loudly, but be sure it doesn't erupt). Maintaining the right temperature is important: too hot, and the onion will scorch from the outside; too low, and you will get a soggy, sad version of this awesome dish.

9|

Place the onion, base down, in the hot oil and fry for 10-12 minutes, or until it turns brown. Carefully remove the onion (remember, this is extra-hot oil) and set aside to drain on a rack for 5 minutes.

10|

If you'd like to increase the guilty pleasure, sprinkle on the bacon bits and grated Cheddar. I love to serve it with the wasabi or jalapeño dipping sauce or both—let the crowd choose. Serve immediately.

Chicken Wings Fest for the Frequent Fly-Higher

Every so often, we need to reset the chicken-wing meter, and I must tell you: gathering up a few buddies and placing among them a few bowls of various sinful chicken wings, accompanied by an assortment of dips, is the way to go. Just grab one of them wings and enjoy them sticky fingers.

A NOTE ABOUT BAKING CHICKEN WINGS:

I find that baking, rather than deep frying, the chicken wings produces a much better taste and texture (not to mention making it easier to clean up afterwards). However, there is one risk: sogginess. To make sure your chicken wings come out crispy, follow these rules:

1|

Use a rack in the pan to allow the fluids to drip. If you don't have a rack, use parchment paper, and make sure to drain the baking pan after roughly 20 minutes of baking. This will discard most of the juices and will prevent the wings from baking in them.

2|

Thoroughly rinse and dry the wings before coating them with the flour. Wrap them in a paper towel and squeeze a bit to remove as much of the dampness as possible.

3|

After coating the wings, place them in an open bowl and refrigerate for 45 minutes.

A TWIST ON THE BUFFALO CLASSIC

2 lb chicken wings

½ cup all-purpose flour

1 tbsp garlic powder

1 tbsp sweet paprika

1 tbsp salt

1 cup barbecue sauce

3 tbsp honey

2 tbsp extra-virgin olive oil

1 tbsp unsalted butter, melted

1 tbsp hot sauce

1|

Wash the chicken wings and pat them dry (see general comment on p. 243).

2|

In a gallon zip-top bag, combine the flour, garlic powder, paprika, and salt. Add the chicken wings, shake well, and set aside to rest in the fridge for an hour.

3|

Preheat the oven to 300°F. Line a baking sheet with a rack or parchment paper.

4|

Remove the chicken wings from the bag and shake off any excess flour. Place the wings on the rack and bake for 1 hour. Remove from the oven.

5|

In a large mixing bowl, combine the barbecue sauce, honey, butter, olive oil, and hot sauce and mix well.

6|

While the baked wings are still steaming hot, add them to the bowl and toss well, until the wings are thoroughly coated.

7|

Return the wings to the baking sheet and bake for another 5 minutes, or until the glaze begins to caramelize. Remove from the oven.

8|

Serve hot.

SUPER-STICKY, EXTRA-CRISPY
WINGS KOREAN STYLE

This one's inspired by Korean cuisine and enjoyed globally. Just make sure you have enough napkins, as it's going to get messy.

2 lb chicken wings

½ cup all-purpose flour

Salt and freshly ground black pepper, to taste

½ cup soy sauce

¼ cup water

3 cloves garlic, minced

1 (½-inch) piece fresh ginger, peeled and grated

2 tbsp honey

1 tbsp red chili pepper flakes

½ tbsp apple cider vinegar or rice vinegar

1 tsp super-finely chopped dried rosemary

1 tsp sesame oil

Chopped scallions, for garnish

White sesame seeds, for garnish

1|

Wash the chicken wings and pat dry with a paper towel (see general comment on p. 243).

2|

In a gallon zip-top bag, combine the flour, salt, and black pepper. Add the chicken wings, shake well, and set aside to rest in the fridge for 1 hour.

3|

Preheat the oven to 400°F. Line a baking sheet with a rack or parchment paper.

4|

Remove the chicken wings from the bag and shake off any excess flour. Place the wings, skin side up, on the rack and bake for 40 minutes, or until they are cooked through and crisp. Remove from the oven.

5|

In a small saucepan over low heat, combine all the remaining ingredients except the scallions and sesame seeds. Whisk to mix well. Once the mixture forms into a sauce, remove from the heat.

6|

Transfer the contents of the saucepan to a large mixing bowl. While the baked wings are still steaming hot, add them to the bowl and toss well, until the wings are thoroughly coated.

7|

Serve immediately garnished with the scallions and sesame seeds.

THE ULTIMATE (CHICKEN) WINGMAN: TRUFFLE AND PARMESAN CRUSTY WINGS

The best advice I can share when considering whether to make this dish: plan to make more... much more. I have a thesis that has so far proven to be fairly accurate. No matter how many of these crispy wings I make, after a few minutes, the plate is empty.

2 lb chicken wings

3 tbsp extra-virgin olive oil

½ cup all-purpose flour

1 tsp salt

1 tsp freshly ground black pepper

½ cup freshly grated Parmesan cheese, plus more
   for topping

3 cloves garlic, finely minced

3 tbsp unsalted butter, melted

1–2 tbsp red chili flakes

1 tsp dried oregano

2 tbsp finely chopped fresh basil leaves, for topping

1|

Wash the chicken wings and pat dry with a paper towel (see general comment on p. 243).

2|

In a mixing bowl, toss the wings with the oil until evenly coated.

3|

In a gallon zip-top bag, combine the flour, salt, and black pepper. Add the chicken wings, shake well, and set aside to rest in the fridge for 1 hour.

4|

Preheat the oven to 400°F. Line a baking sheet with a rack or parchment paper.

5|

Remove the chicken wings from the bag and shake off any excess flour. Place the wings, skin side up, on the rack and bake for 40 minutes.

6|

Raise the oven temperature to broil and broil the wings for another 3 minutes (and no more). Remove from the oven.

7|

In a large mixing bowl, whisk together all the remaining ingredients except the basil. While the baked wings are still steaming hot, add them to the bowl and toss well, until the wings are thoroughly coated.

8|

Return the wings to the baking sheet and broil for another 5 minutes, or until the Parmesan starts darkening (it's important to allow enough time for the chicken wings to get crispy; otherwise they might feel a bit soggy). Remove from the oven.

9|

Serve immediately sprinkled with the basil and more of the Parmesan.

Moderate   *20min*   *Meaty*

THE ULTIMATE STACKED TUNA MELT

My wife, Daphne, is a tuna melt fan. But whenever I deviate from the classic way of doing things, she typically dismisses my attempts as being unnecessarily complicated. I obviously couldn't give it a rest, so I took it upon myself to work tirelessly to design a tuna melt that stays true to its classic roots but still provides a delightful culinary twist. It worked!

1

1 (5 oz) can albacore tuna in olive oil

1 small stalk celery, finely chopped

¼ cup finely diced red onion

Freshly squeezed juice of lemon

1 tbsp finely chopped jalapeño pepper

1 tbsp good-quality mayonnaise

1 tsp ground fresh horseradish

½ tsp Dijon mustard

Salt and freshly ground black pepper, to taste

2 tbsp unsalted butter, softened

3 slices sourdough bread

2 slices Cheddar or Gruyère cheese

½ cup roughly chopped arugula leaves

½ cup roughly chopped roasted red peppers

4 toothpicks

1|

In a mixing bowl, combine the tuna, celery, red onion, lemon juice, jalapeño pepper, mayonnaise, horseradish, and mustard. Mix well until it reaches an even consistency and season with the salt and black pepper.

2|

Spread most of the butter on 1 side of all 3 bread slices and also on the other side of the slice you designate to be the middle layer.

3|

Warm a pan over medium heat. Add the bread slices, buttered sides down, and sear for about 3 minutes. These sides will be the ones "facing" the food; searing them prevents the bread from getting too soggy. Remove from the heat.

4|

Butter the two remaining unbuttered sides of the bread slices. Place 1 slice, buttered side down, on a clean cutting board. Add ½ of the tuna mixture and place a cheese slice on top of it. Scatter over the arugula leaves. Then add the middle slice of bread and again add the remaining tuna, the second cheese slice, and the red peppers. Close it off with the remaining slice, buttered side up.

5|

Stick 4 toothpicks in the sandwich to ensure this beauty doesn't collapse when you're heating it up.

6|

Return the pan to low-medium heat and place the entire sandwich, freshly buttered side down, in the pan. Place a spatula or a small pot of water on top to weigh down the stack and cook until the lower cheese slice starts melting. Then, quickly turn the sandwich over and cook for a few minutes on that side as well. This is the most delicate part; if the heat is too high, you might char the bread slices... so pay attention. Remove from the heat.

7|

With the toothpicks still in, cut the sandwich in half and eat up.

Simple   25min   Meaty

LOADED NACHOS GALORE

You can't have a cannabis-infused cookbook with a chapter focused on guilty savory pleasures and not have adequate representation of a loaded nachos delight. Maybe you're a college student, or maybe those days are behind you and you just want to indulge in a nostalgic culinary retrospective—whichever it is, you're bound to enjoy.

8

3 tbsp canola oil, plus more as needed

1 large onion, diced

1 green pepper, cut into thin strips

1 red pepper, cut into thin strips

1 lb sirloin steak, cubed

2 garlic cloves, minced

1 tbsp cayenne pepper

¼ tsp dried oregano

1 tsp ground cumin

½ tsp ground coriander

½ tsp sweet or smoked paprika

Salt and freshly ground black pepper, to taste

5 cups tortilla chips

1½ cups freshly grated provolone cheese

1 cup freshly grated mozzarella cheese

1 large tomato, diced, for garnish

1 avocado, peeled, pitted and diced, for garnish

3 scallions, finely chopped, for garnish

1|

Preheat the oven to 350°F.

2|

In a heavy pan over high heat, warm the oil. Add the onions and sauté for 4 to 5 minutes, or until they become translucent. Add the peppers and sauté, stirring frequently, for another 3 minutes.

3|

Using a wooden spoon, push the vegetables to the edges of the hot pan and add the steak cubes to the center. If needed, add another tablespoon of oil to make sure the meat doesn't stick. Cook, stirring occasionally, for 5 minutes, or until the steak is lightly charred; be careful not to overcook, as the meat will quickly dry out.

4|

Add the garlic, cayenne pepper, oregano, cumin, smoked paprika, and coriander and season with the salt and black pepper. Cook, stirring constantly, for another 2 minutes, or until evenly mixed. Remove from the heat.

5|

Cover a baking sheet with a third of the tortilla chips. Add a third of the contents of the pan and sprinkle over a third of the cheeses. Repeat with another layer of each, and then repeat again. Bake for 10-15 minutes, or until the cheese melts and scorches just a bit. Remove from the oven.

6|

Serve garnished with the tomatoes, scallions, and avocado. Add some spicy sauces, if you're into that. It's best to eat this with some sour cream and guacamole (see p. 165).

Moderate   15min   Meaty

PB&J INSPIRED BY THE KING

Elvis Presley, "the King," used to eat this sandwich after shows. For those of you who appreciate the music (and for those who have yet to learn to appreciate…) I'd recommend giving a chance to this dish as it will create a whole symphony of salty and sweet music in your mouth.

 1

2 slices bacon

2 tbsp strawberry or grape jam

1 tbsp cream cheese

2 thick slices white bread

2 tbsp smooth peanut butter

½ banana, cut into thin slices

9 toothpicks

1|

Place the bacon strips on a cold pan and place over low heat. Let the bacon cook until it curls up and chars. Using tongs, loosen the bacon strips and turn to cook on the other side. When it's crusty on both sides, remove the bacon from the pan and place on a plate lined with a paper towel to drain. Remove from the heat but don't drain the bacon fat—we'll use it soon enough.

2|

Spread the jam and the cream cheese on one of the bread slices and the peanut butter on the other.

3|

Layer the banana slices and the bacon strips on the slices of bread. I like to put the banana on the peanut butter-coated slice and then add the bacon strips. Then, I close it down with the cream cheese and jelly bread slice. This way you get salty-sweet-salty-sweet combo.

4|

Return the pan to low-medium heat and, once the bacon fat is nice and hot, place the sandwich in the pan. Fry on both sides until the bread turns beautifully golden and crusty. Remove from the heat and pat dry with paper towels.

5|

Evenly stick the toothpicks into the sandwich and, using a sharp knife, cut the sandwich into 9 squares, each of which is held by a toothpick. Serve warm. This is best eaten with some Elvis tunes playing in the background.

Moderate   80min   Vegetarian

LOADED SWEET POTATO SKINS

This is a game-day favorite in our household: it gives you either that extra wind you need to cheer for your team, or that most-necessary comfort in the event your team finds itself on the wrong side of winning.

6

4 medium sweet potatoes

4 slices thick-cut bacon

1½ cups shredded Mexican cheese mix

1 tomato, cut into small cubes

½ cup chopped walnuts

¼ jalapeño pepper, finely chopped

3 tbsp heavy cream or half-and-half

1 clove garlic, minced

1 tsp sweet paprika

Extra-virgin olive oil, for drizzling

½ avocado, peeled, pitted, and sliced into small cubes

½ cup sour cream

½ cup finely chopped fresh chives, for garnish

Salt and freshly ground black pepper, to taste

1|
Preheat the oven to 350°F.

2|
Wash the sweet potatoes thoroughly. Pat them dry, wrap them in aluminum foil, and place them on a baking sheet. Bake for 1 hour, or until fork tender.

3|
Cut the sweet potatoes in half and set aside to cool for 5 to 10 minutes.

4|
Place the bacon strips on a cold pan and place over low heat. Let the bacon cook until it curls up and chars. Using tongs, loosen the bacon strips and turn to cook on the other side. When it's crusty on both sides, remove the strips from the pan and place them on a plate lined with a paper towel to drain. Remove from the heat.

5|
Finely chop the bacon. Set aside.

6|
Using a spoon, scrape the sweet potato meat out of the peels, leaving a layer inside the skins that's thick enough to allow them to stand on their own.

7|
In a mixing bowl, combine the sweet potato meat and half of the shredded cheese. Add the tomato, walnuts, jalapeño pepper, cream, garlic, and paprika and stir until well combined.

8|
Coat the sweet potato skins with a drizzle of the oil, return them to the baking sheet, and bake for about 5 minutes to get them a bit crispier. Remove from the oven.

9|
Fill each skin with the sweet potato mixture and top with the chopped bacon, the remaining shredded cheese, and the avocado. Return to the oven and bake until the cheese has completely melted and darkened just a bit. Remove from the oven.

10|
Transfer the baked sweet potato skins to a plate and add a generous tablespoon of the sour cream to each. Garnish with the chives, and black pepper and dig in.

Advanced 25min Vegetarian

CHOCOLATE FONDANT FOR SOARING EXPLORERS

This one's a karma-boosting delicacy. I love seeing the childlike, joyful expressions on my friends' faces when I bring this out. There are very few things in life that make people with the munchies happier than a hot, liquid chocolate fondant alongside the customary vanilla ice cream.

9 small soufflé molds

½ lb unsalted butter

2 tbsp cocoa powder, plus more for sprinkling

7 oz (200g) dark chocolate (72% and above)

1 tbsp Tabasco sauce (optional)

1 cup confectioners' sugar, plus more for sprinkling

4 whole large eggs

4 large egg yolks

½ tsp vanilla extract

Dash salt

1 cup all-purpose flour

High-quality vanilla ice cream, for serving

1|

Preheat the oven to 350°F.

2|

First, get the soufflé molds in order. Melt 3 tbsp of the butter in the microwave in 20-second bursts until it is completely liquified. Generously brush the molds with the butter.

3|

Pour the cocoa powder into one of the molds and tip it sideways to ensure it is coated. Pour the excess cocoa powder into the next mold and so on until all of the molds are evenly coated.

4|

Break up the dark chocolate into cubes and cut up the remaining butter into ½-inch-wide pieces. If you like a spicy kick, this is the time to add the Tabasco. Combine the chocolate, butter, and Tabasco, if using, in a microwavable bowl and melt the mixture in 20-second intervals, stirring in between each interval.

5|

In a mixing bowl, whisk together the sugar, eggs, yolks, vanilla extract, and salt until the mixture becomes thick. Add the flour and slowly stir together just until the mixture is even.

6|

Using a spatula, slowly and gradually add the melted chocolate mixture into the egg and flour mixture. Fold the mixture together until it reaches an even consistency.

7|

Divide the batter evenly among the molds and place them in the oven. Bake for 12 minutes, or until the tops form a delicate crust. Remove from the oven and set aside to cool for a few minutes.

8|

Gently loosen the fondants and place each of them on serving plates. Sprinkle a little extra cocoa powder and confectioners' sugar over each of them and add a hefty serving of ice cream to each serving.

Moderate   *15min*   *Vegetarian**

MARSHMALLOW, RICE KRISPIES, AND OREO MILKSHAKE

This super-sweet and indulgent shake is for those who like mixing their highs with a sugar rush.

 4

1 tbsp hot water

¼ cup + 1 tbsp granulated sugar

1 cup marshmallows

3 cups vanilla ice cream

1 cup Rice Krispies

½ cup whole milk

8 Oreo cookies

1|

In a measuring cup, whisk together the water and sugar until all the sugar is dissolved. This might take more than a minute, as you're trying to make a very condensed syrup.

2|

In a microwave-safe bowl, combine the marshmallows and your newly created syrup and zap on high for 20 seconds. Remove from the microwave and mix thoroughly: the marshmallows will start melting, but there will still be some solid pieces.

3|

Add the milk and zap on high in 10-second intervals, mixing thoroughly in between each, until the mixture has a smooth, runny texture.

4|

In the jug of a blender, combine the marshmallow mixture, ice cream, Rice Krispies, and milk, along with 6 of the Oreo cookies. Blend until the mixture reaches an even consistency.

5|

Pour into milkshake glasses and garnish with the remaining Oreo cookies.

Contains gelatin.

15 Important Periods in Cannabis History

1   **2737 BC**   The first recorded use of cannabis as medication for gout, rheumatism, malaria, and other maladies by the Chinese emperor Shen Neng.

2   **800 BC**   "Bhang" is mentioned in Hindu sacred texts as a substance used for medicinal, ritual, and recreational purposes.

3   **130–200 AD**   Galen, a Greek physician, prescribes hemp cakes to promote the feeling of well-being, though he did mention that taken to excess, they lead to intoxication.

4   **1200**   The famous Arabian tale *One Thousand and One Nights* describes hashish as an intoxicating and soothing substance.

5   **1621**   Marijuana is suggested as a potential treatment for depression in Burton's *Anatomy of Melancholy*.

6   **1850**   Cannabis is added to the US Pharmacopoeia—for the next 65 years marijuana could easily be purchased throughout the US in pharmacies.

7   **1913**   Prohibition begins in the US, with California banning the use of cannabis. This was followed on a national scale in the years to come.

8   **1936**   The propaganda film *Reefer Madness* is released with the express purpose of scaring American youths away from consuming weed.

9   **1937**   The Marijuana Tax Act is introduced, effectively prohibiting cannabis in the US at the federal level.

10   **1941**   Cannabis is removed from the US Pharmacopoeia, and its medicinal use is no longer recognized.

11   **1951**   Mandatory sentences for marijuana possession and consumption are introduced in the US.

12   **1976**   The Netherlands adopts a formal policy of non-enforcement, which de facto permits users to legally possess 30 g or less of marijuana.

13   **1996**   California is the first US state to legalize medical marijuana to treat serious illnesses. This practice is followed by other states as well.

14   **2012**   The US states of Colorado and Washington legalize marijuana for recreational use. In 2014, Seattle becomes the first city in which marijuana is sold over the counter. More states followed in subsequent years.

15   **2020**   The book *High Cookery* is first introduced, and the world is happy.